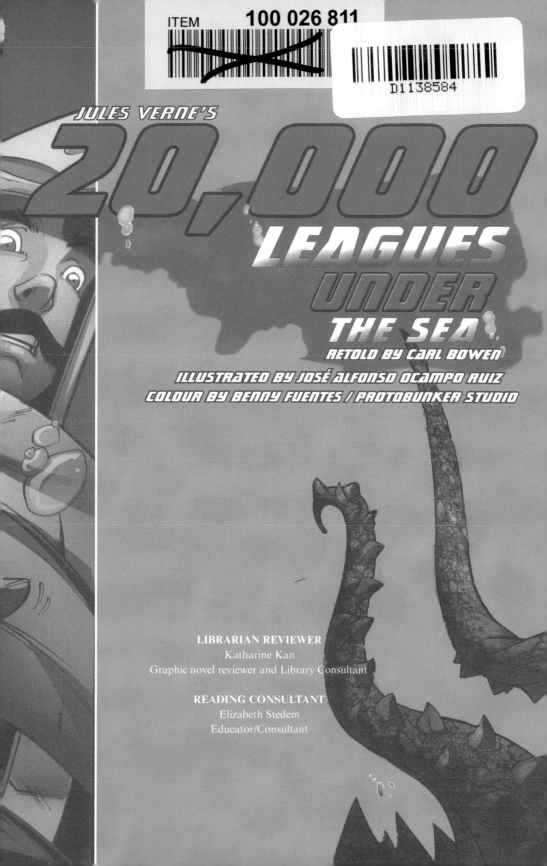

JULES VERNE'S

20,000 LEAGUES UNDER THE SEA

RETOLD BY CARL BOWEN

ILLUSTRATED BY JOSÉ ALFONSO OCAMPO RUIZ
COLOUR BY BENNY FUENTES / PROTOBUNKER STUDIO

LIBRARIAN REVIEWER
Katharine Kan
Graphic novel reviewer and Library Consultant

READING CONSULTANT
Elizabeth Stedem
Educator/Consultant

www.raintreepublishers.co.uk
Visit our website to find out
more information about
Raintree books.

To order:
☎ Phone +44 (0) 1865 888066
🖷 Fax +44 (0) 1865 314091
💻 Visit www.raintreepublishers.co.uk

Raintree is an imprint of Capstone Global Library Limited, a company incorporated in
England and Wales having its registered office at 7 Pilgrim Street, London, EC4V 6LB –
Registered company number: 6695582

"Raintree" is a registered trademark of Pearson Education Limited, under licence to
Capstone Global Library Limited

Text © Stone Arch Books, 2009
First published by Stone Arch Books in 2008
First published in hardback in the United Kingdom in 2009

The moral rights of the proprietor have been asserted.

Art Director: Heather Kindseth
Graphic Designer: Kay Fraser
Color by Benny Fuentes and Protobunker Studio
Edited in the UK by Laura Knowles
Printed and bound in the United Kingdom

ISBN 978-1406212532 (hardback)
ISBN 978-1406213553 (paperback)
13 12 11 10 09
10 9 8 7 6 5 4 3 2 1

British Library Cataloguing in Publication Data
Bowen, Carl.
20,000 leagues under the sea. -- (Graphic revolve)
741.5-dc22
A full catalogue record for this book is available from the British Library.

TABLE OF CONTENTS

INTRODUCING
(Cast of Characters) 4

CHAPTER 1:
The Hunt Begins 6

CHAPTER 2:
Inside the *Nautilus* 16

CHAPTER 3:
Death at Sea 24

CHAPTER 4:
Underwater Adventures 32

CHAPTER 5:
The Voyage Ends 55

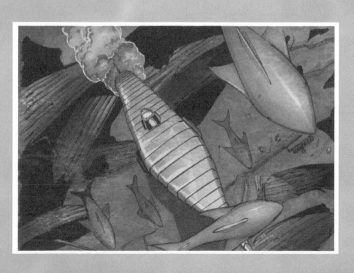

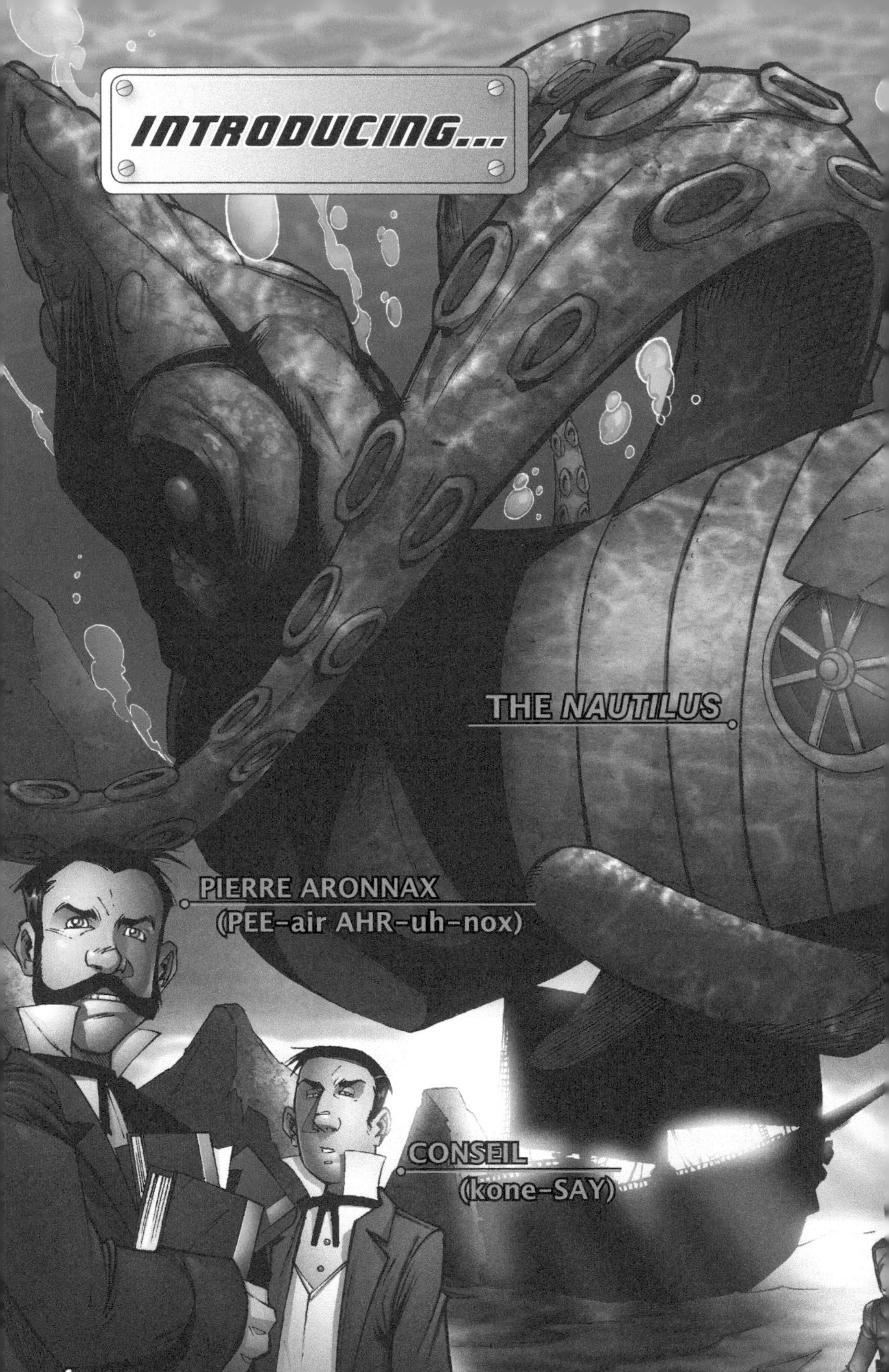
INTRODUCING...
THE NAUTILUS
PIERRE ARONNAX
(PEE-air AHR-uh-nox)
CONSEIL
(kone-SAY)

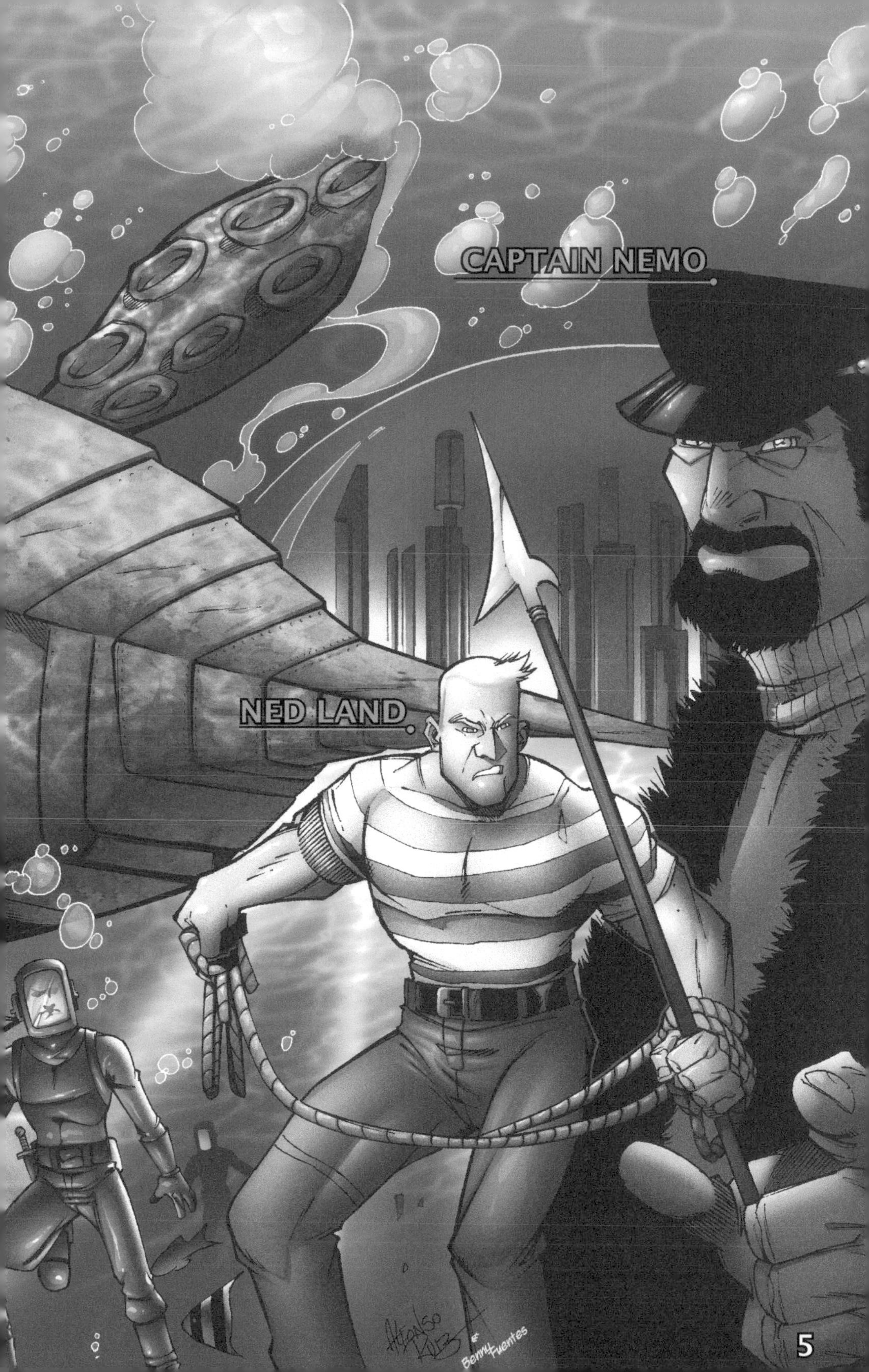
CAPTAIN NEMO
NED LAND

CHAPTER 1: The Hunt Begins

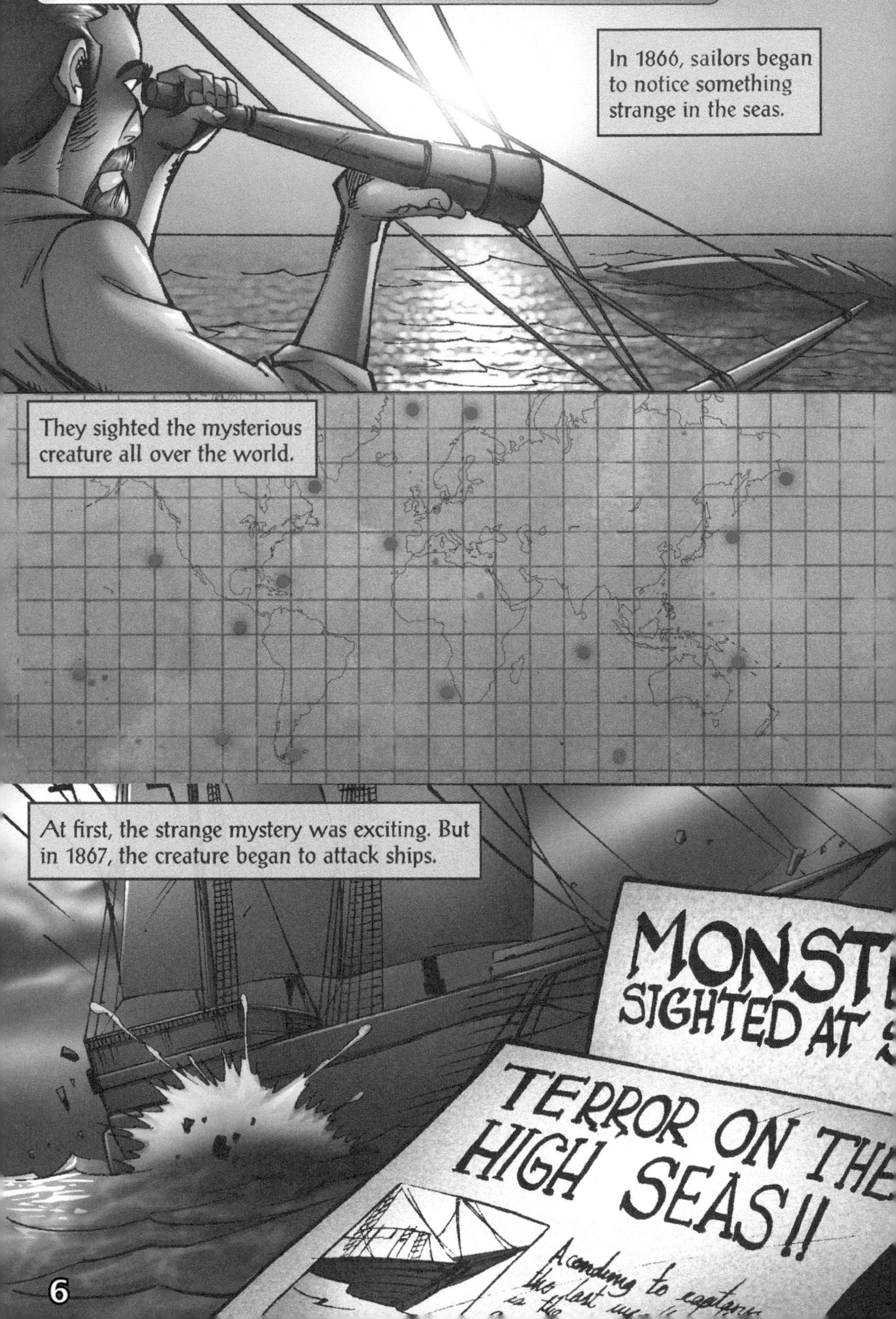

In 1866, sailors began to notice something strange in the seas.
They sighted the mysterious creature all over the world.
At first, the strange mystery was exciting. But in 1867, the creature began to attack ships.
SIGHTED AT
TERROR ON THE HIGH SEAS!!

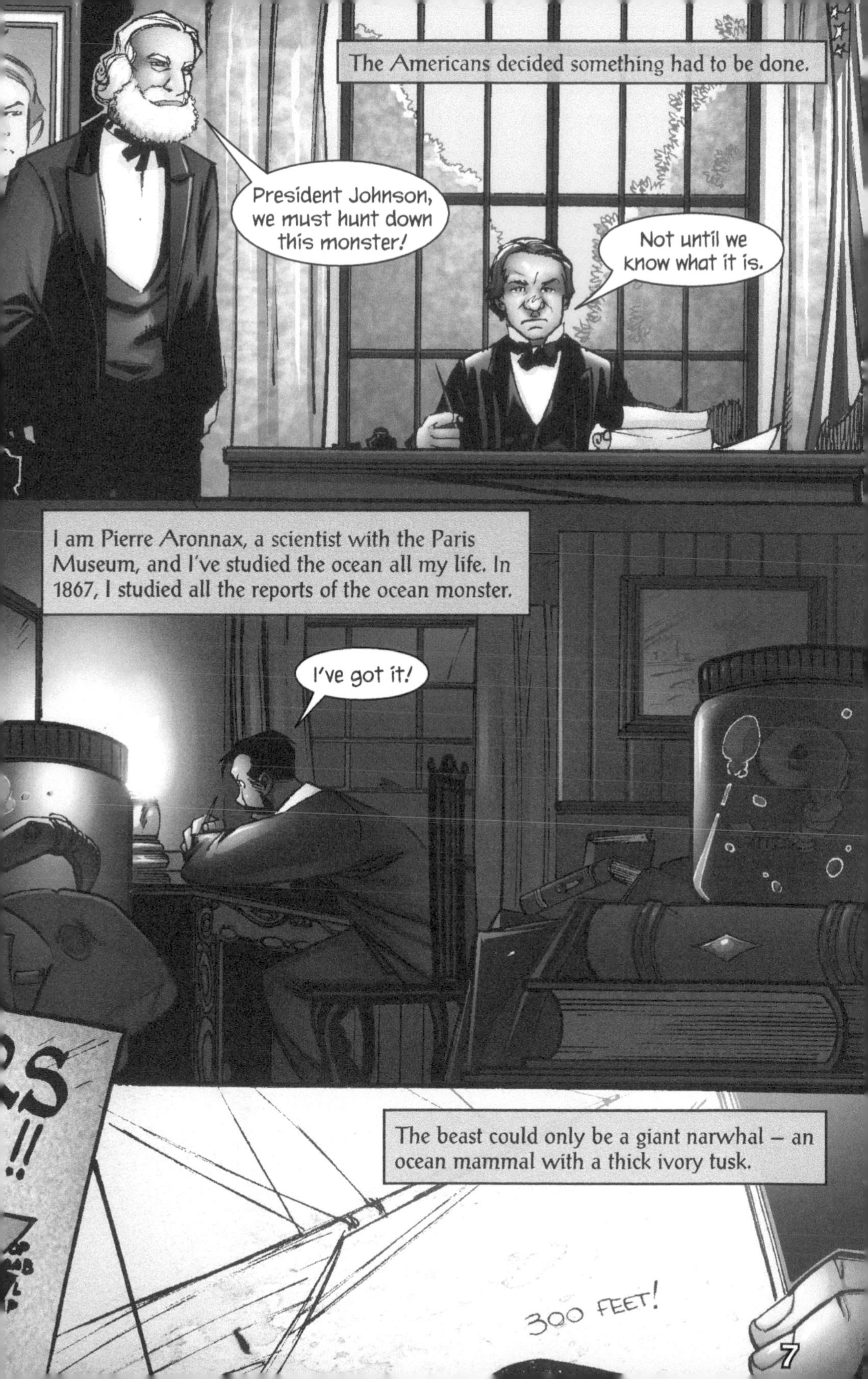

The Americans decided something had to be done.
President Johnson, we must hunt down this monster!
Not until we know what it is.
I am Pierre Aronnax, a scientist with the Paris Museum, and I've studied the ocean all my life. In 1867, I studied all the reports of the ocean monster.
I've got it!
The beast could only be a giant narwhal – an ocean mammal with a thick ivory tusk.
300 FEET!

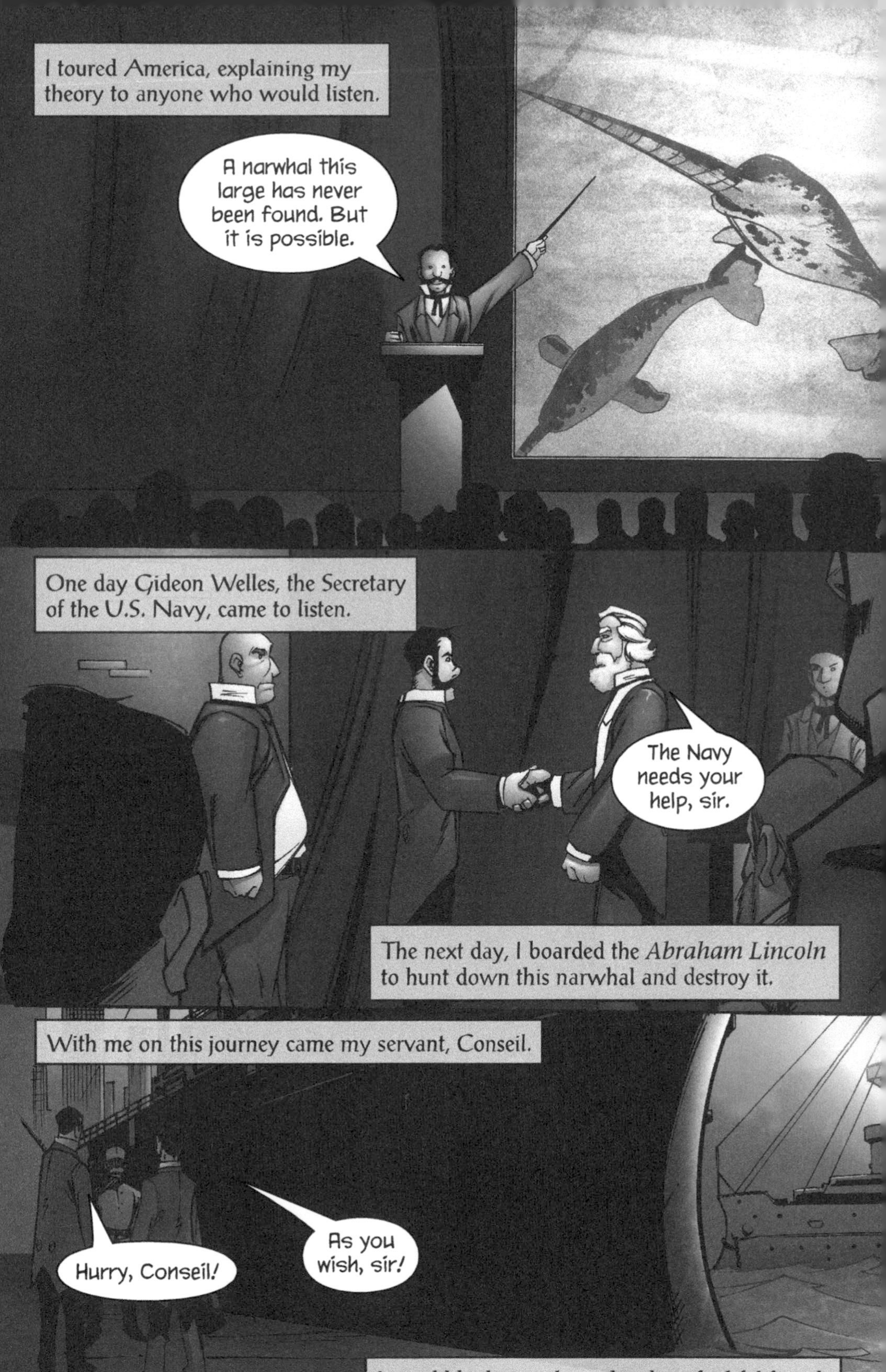
I toured America, explaining my theory to anyone who would listen.
A narwhal this large has never been found. But it is possible.
One day Gideon Welles, the Secretary of the U.S. Navy, came to listen.
The Navy needs your help, sir.
The next day, I boarded the *Abraham Lincoln* to hunt down this narwhal and destroy it.
With me on this journey came my servant, Conseil.
Hurry, Conseil!
As you wish, sir!
I would be lost without this dear, faithful friend.

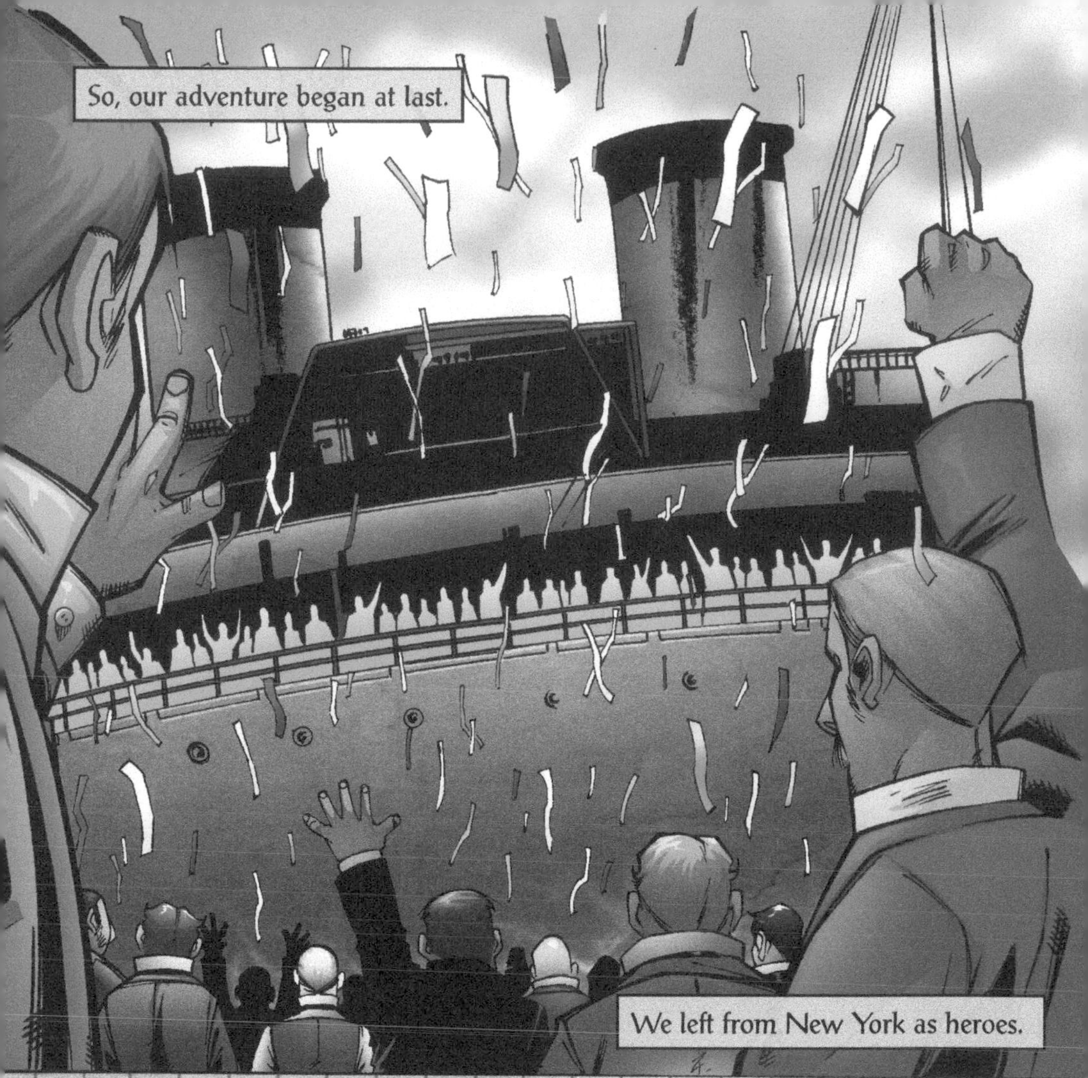
So, our adventure began at last.
We left from New York as heroes.

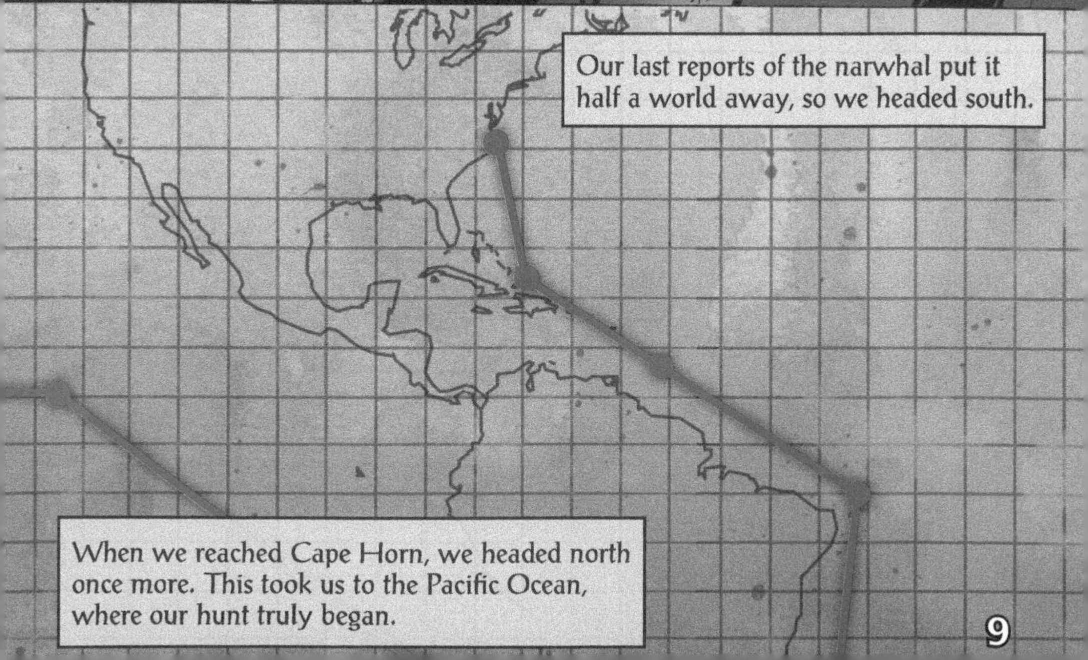
Our last reports of the narwhal put it half a world away, so we headed south.
When we reached Cape Horn, we headed north once more. This took us to the Pacific Ocean, where our hunt truly began.

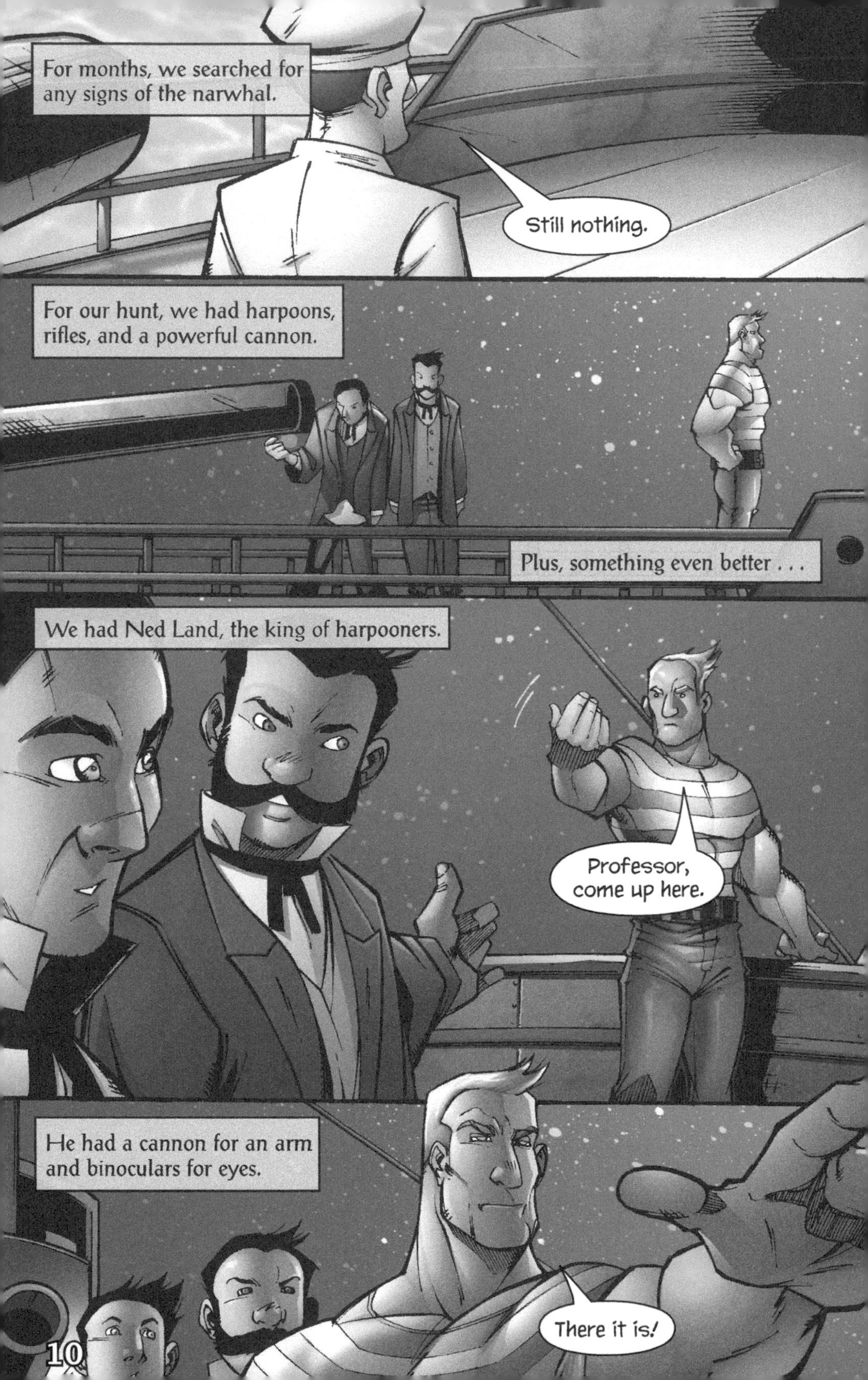
For months, we searched for any signs of the narwhal.
Still nothing.
For our hunt, we had harpoons, rifles, and a powerful cannon.
Plus, something even better . . .
We had Ned Land, the king of harpooners.
Professor, come up here.
He had a cannon for an arm and binoculars for eyes.
There it is!

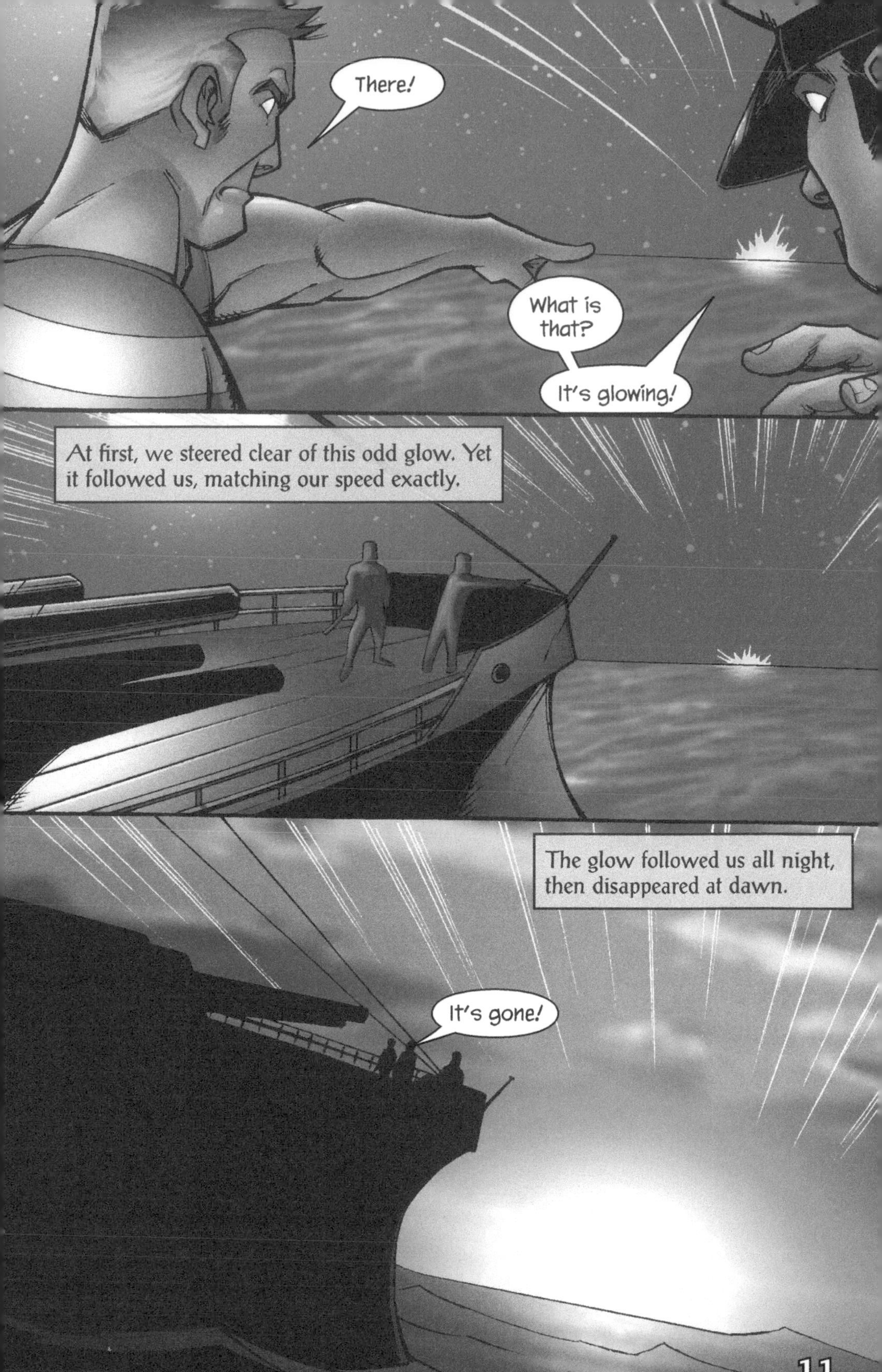
There!
What is that?
It's glowing!
At first, we steered clear of this odd glow. Yet it followed us, matching our speed exactly.
The glow followed us all night, then disappeared at dawn.
It's gone!

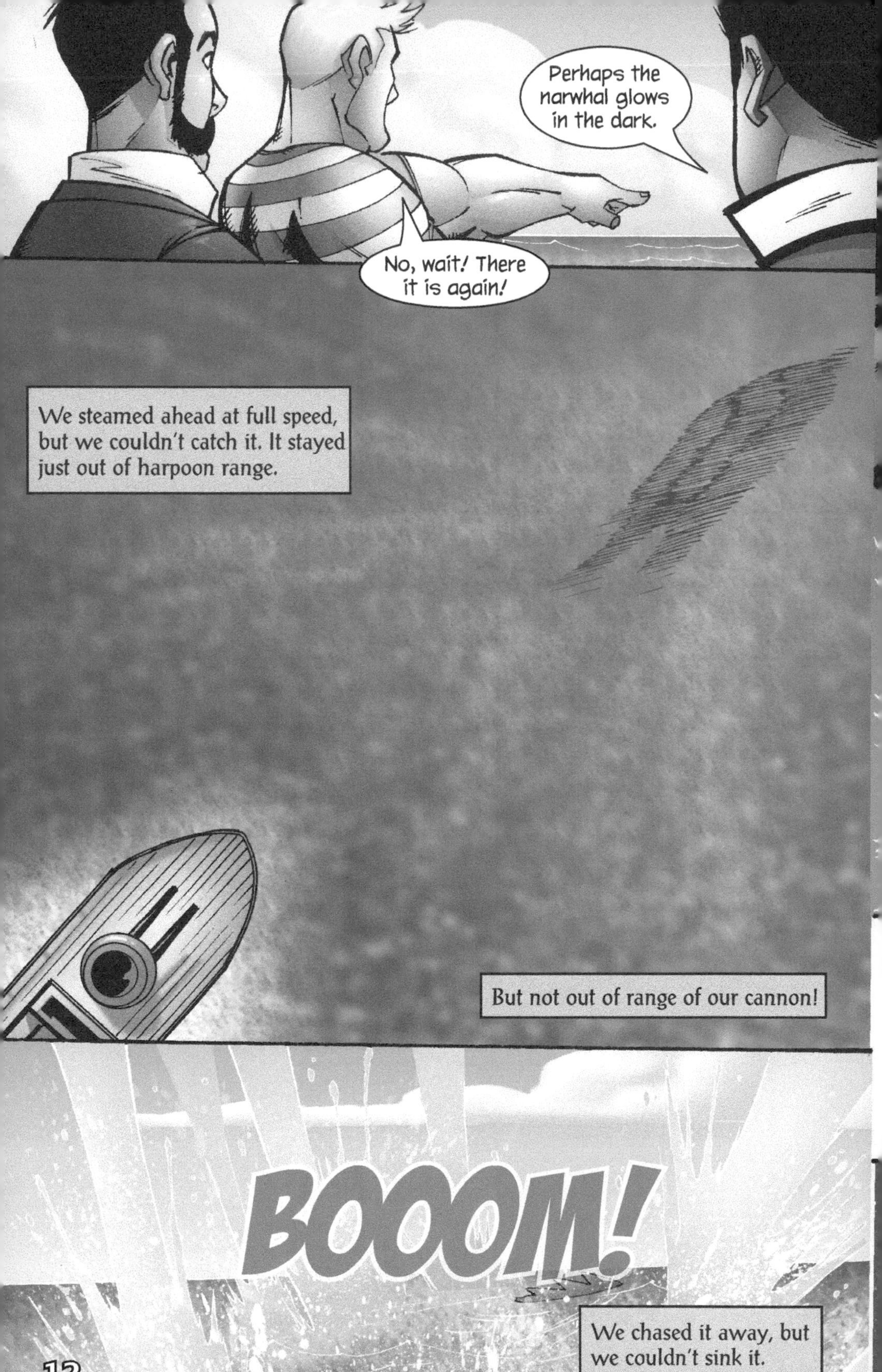
Perhaps the narwhal glows in the dark.
No, wait! There it is again!
We steamed ahead at full speed, but we couldn't catch it. It stayed just out of harpoon range.
But not out of range of our cannon!
BOOOM!
We chased it away, but we couldn't sink it.

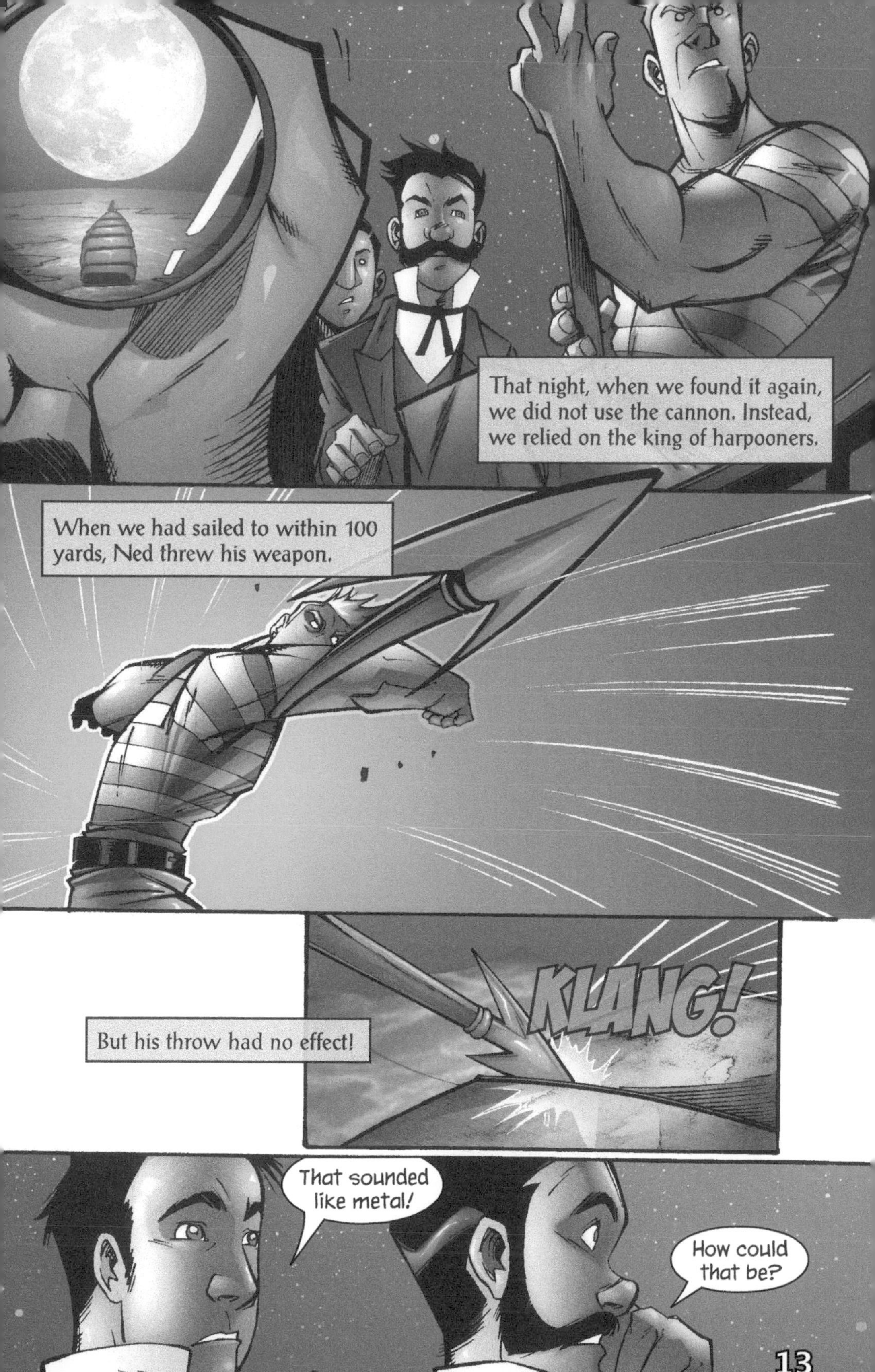
That night, when we found it again, we did not use the cannon. Instead, we relied on the king of harpooners.
When we had sailed to within 100 yards, Ned threw his weapon.
But his throw had no effect!
KLANG!
That sounded like metal!
How could that be?

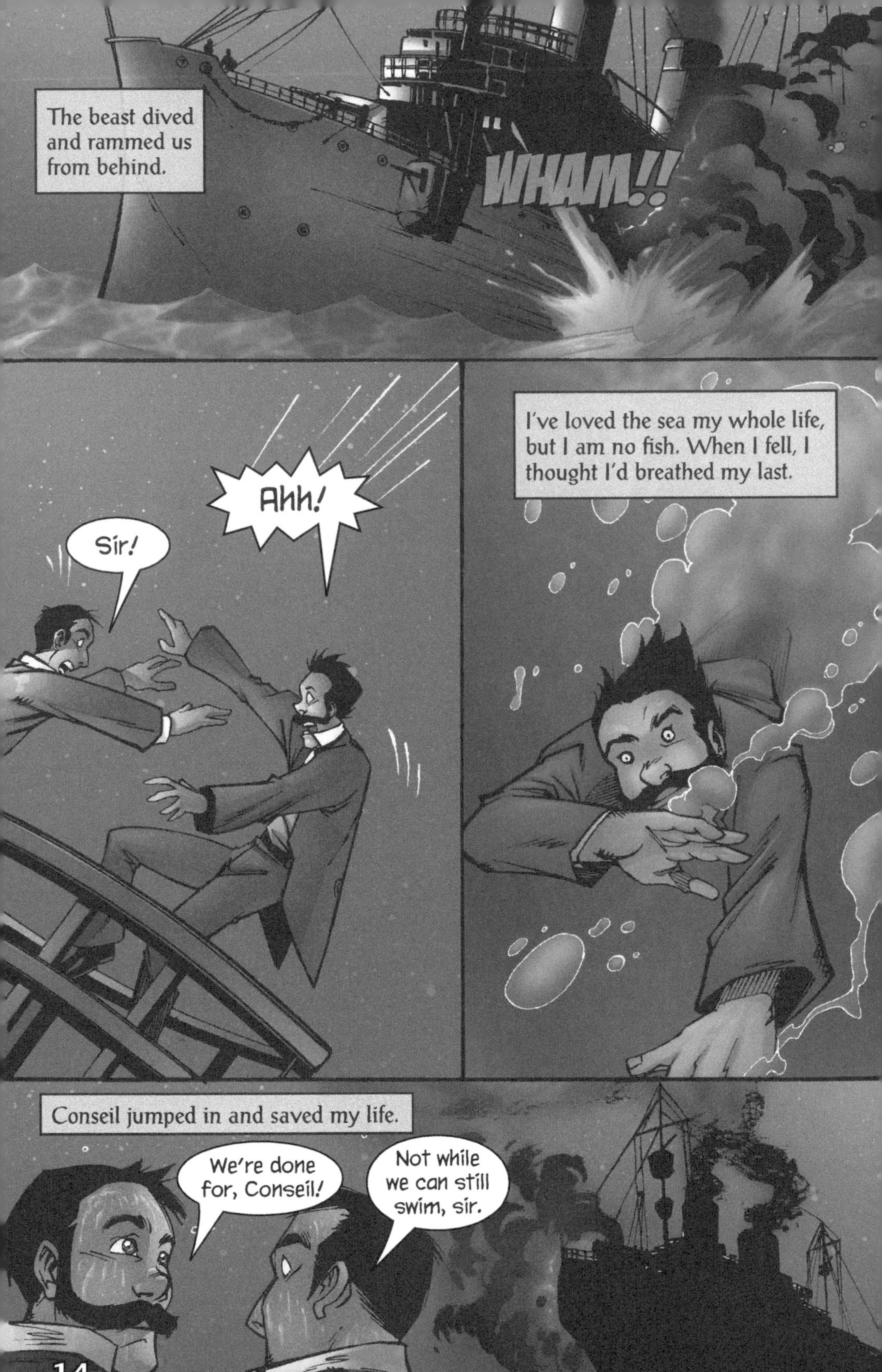
The beast dived and rammed us from behind.
WHAM!!
Sir!
Ahh!
I've loved the sea my whole life, but I am no fish. When I fell, I thought I'd breathed my last.
Conseil jumped in and saved my life.
We're done for, Conseil!
Not while we can still swim, sir.

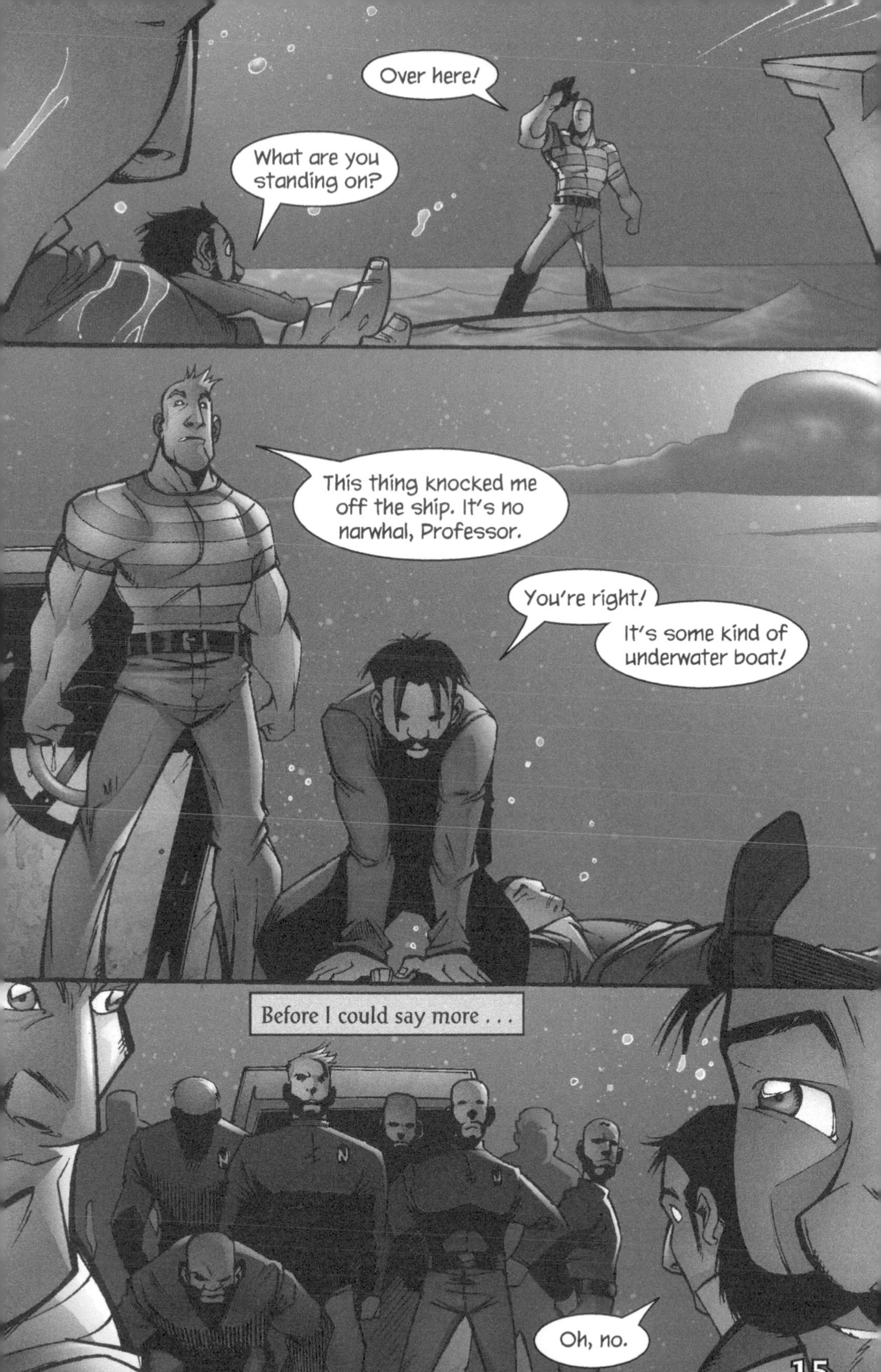
Over here!
What are you standing on?
This thing knocked me off the ship. It's no narwhal, Professor.
You're right!
It's some kind of underwater boat!
Before I could say more . . .
Oh, no.

CHAPTER 2: Inside the *Nautilus*

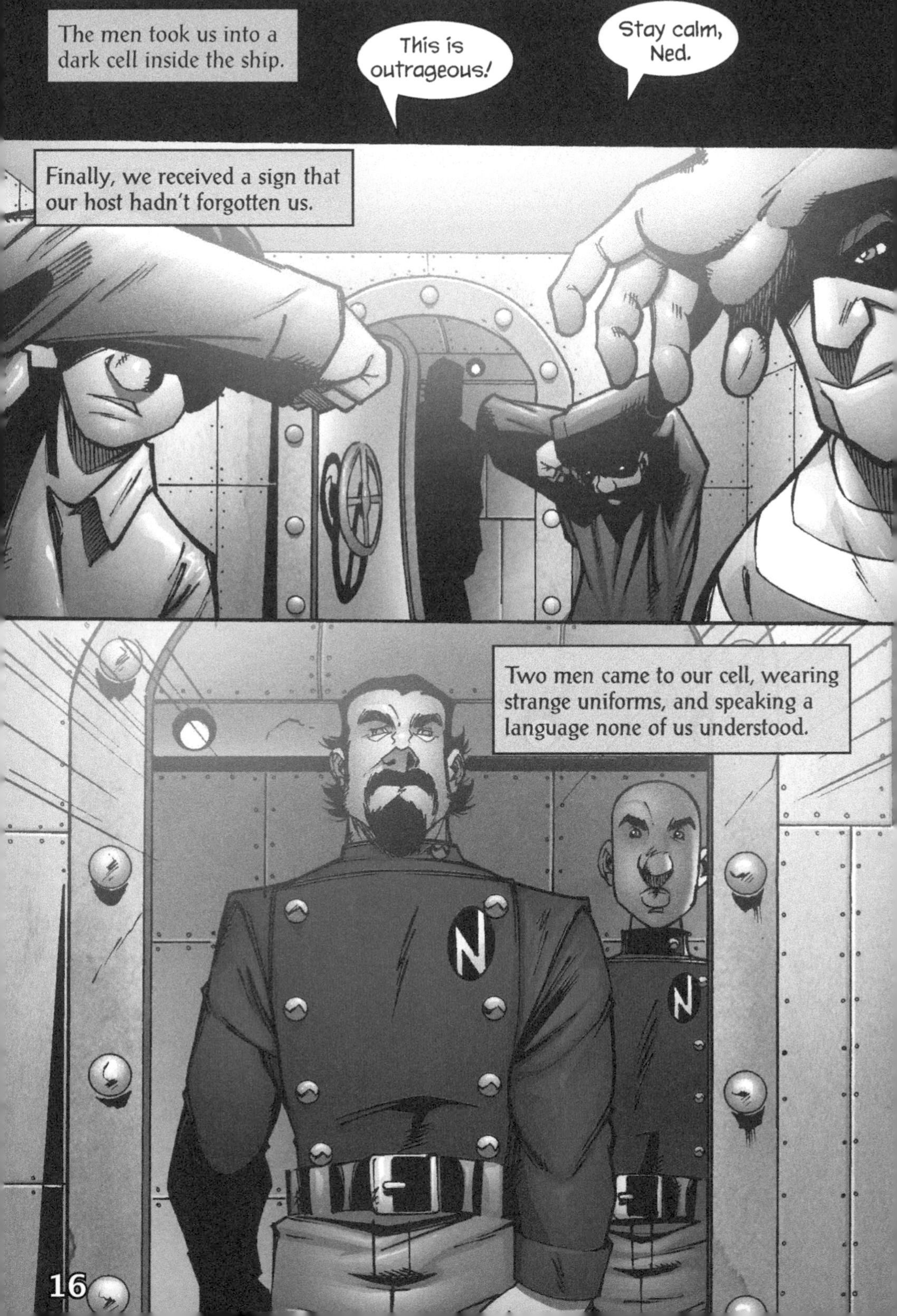

The men took us into a dark cell inside the ship.
This is outrageous!
Stay calm, Ned.
Finally, we received a sign that our host hadn't forgotten us.
Two men came to our cell, wearing strange uniforms, and speaking a language none of us understood.

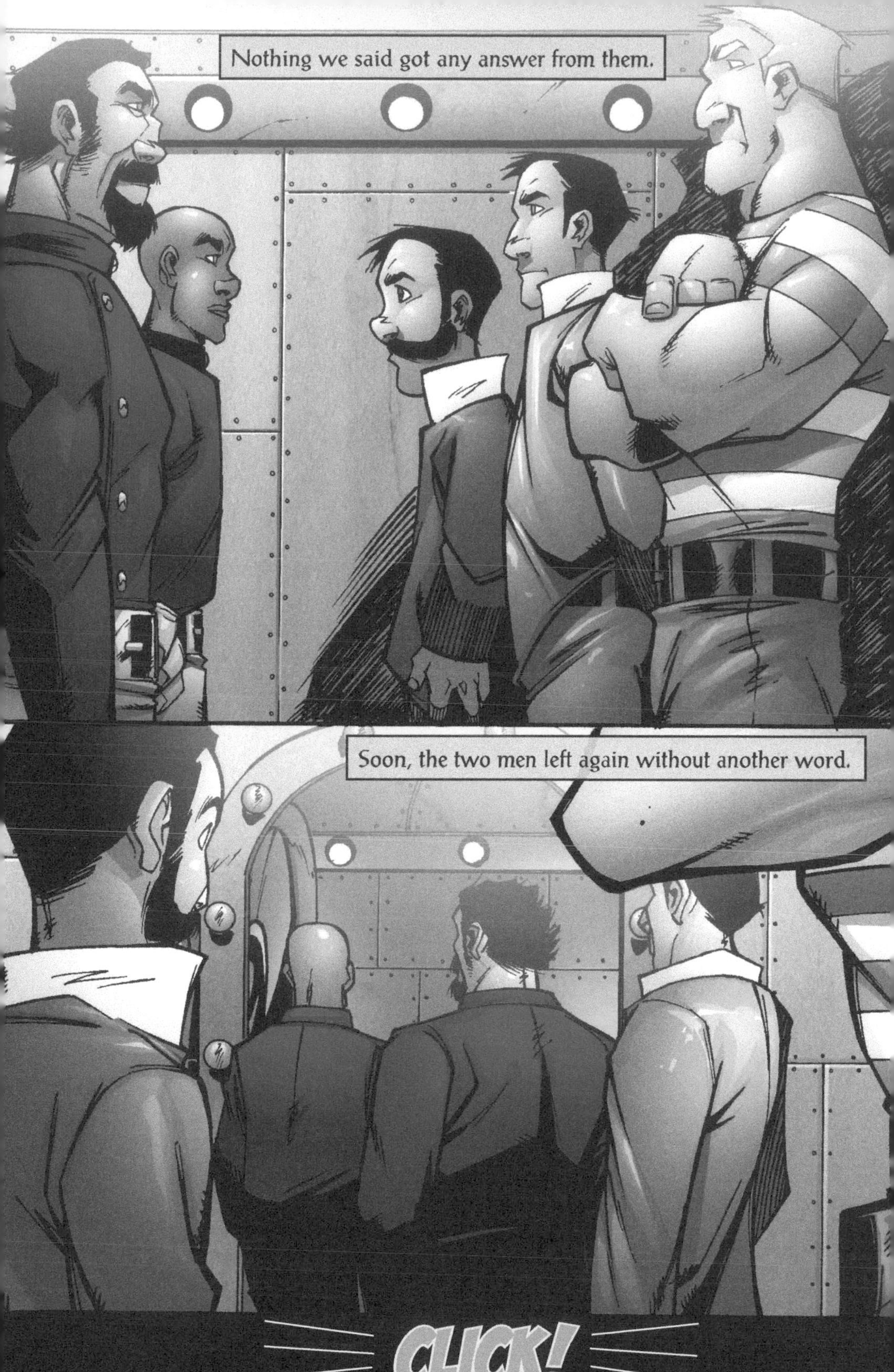
Nothing we said got any answer from them.
Soon, the two men left again without another word.
CLICK!

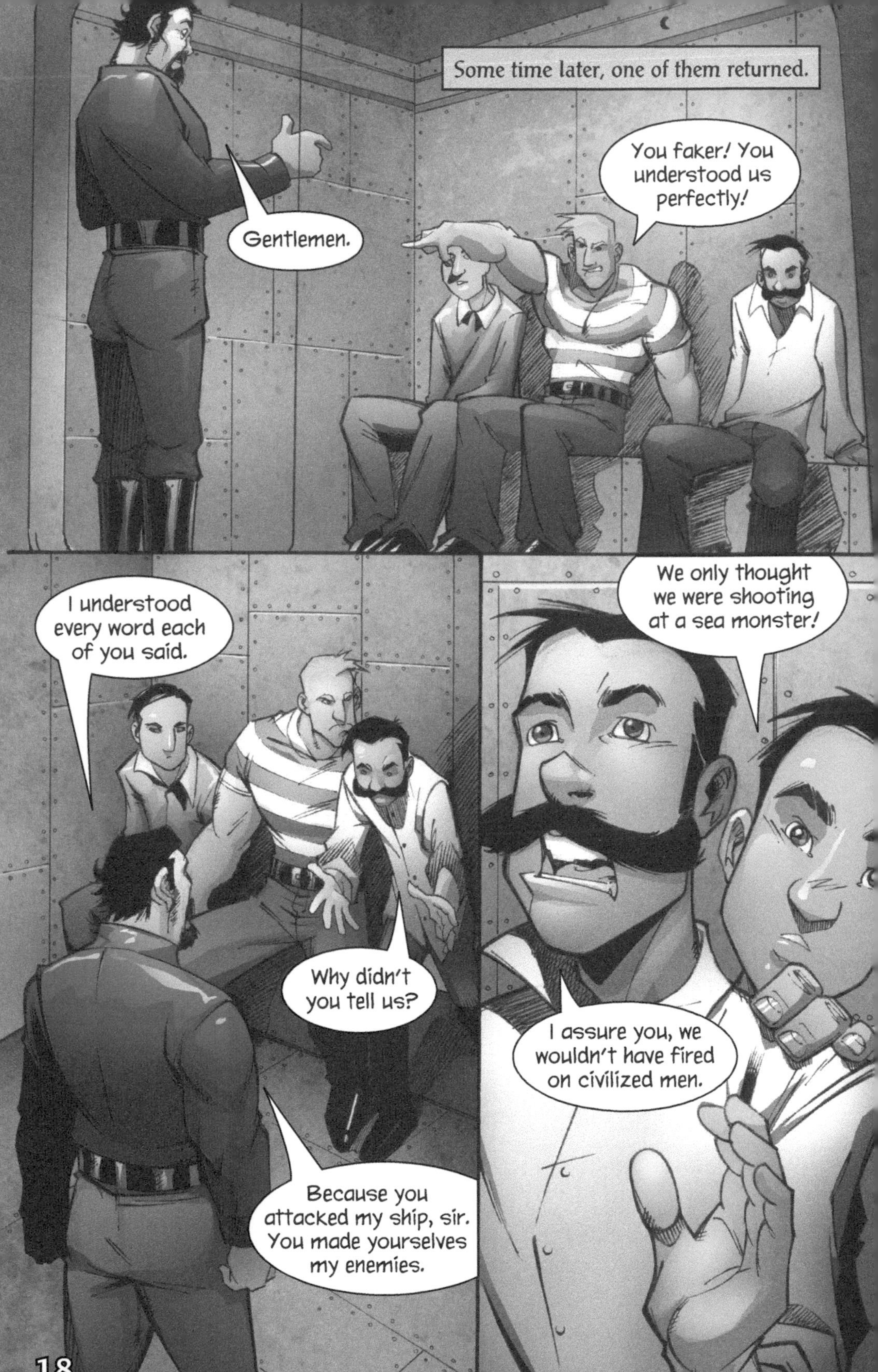
Some time later, one of them returned.
Gentlemen.
You faker! You understood us perfectly!
I understood every word each of you said.
Why didn't you tell us?
Because you attacked my ship, sir. You made yourselves my enemies.
We only thought we were shooting at a sea monster!
I assure you, we wouldn't have fired on civilized men.

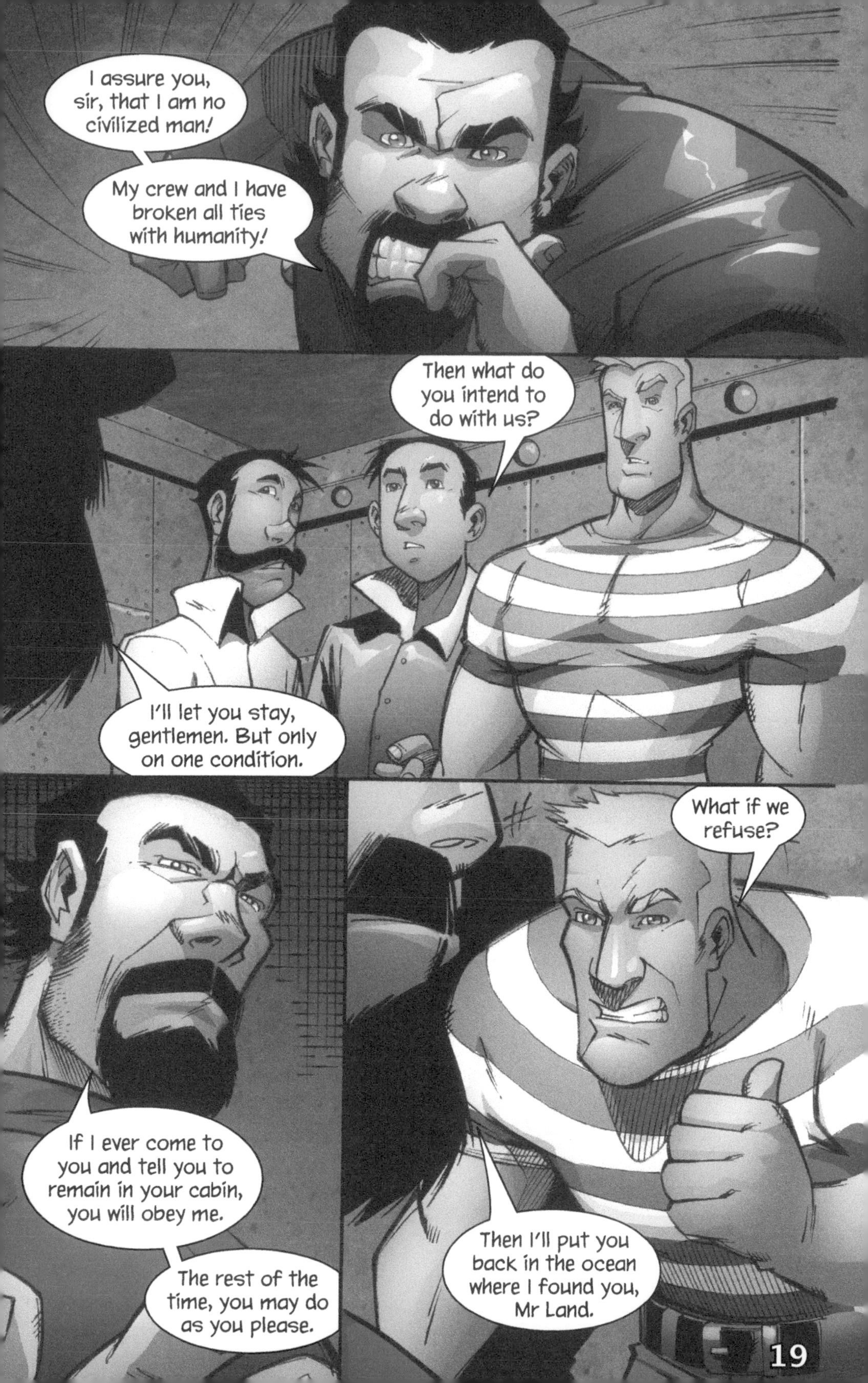
I assure you, sir, that I am no civilized man!
My crew and I have broken all ties with humanity!
Then what do you intend to do with us?
I'll let you stay, gentlemen. But only on one condition.
If I ever come to you and tell you to remain in your cabin, you will obey me.
The rest of the time, you may do as you please.
What if we refuse?
Then I'll put you back in the ocean where I found you, Mr Land.

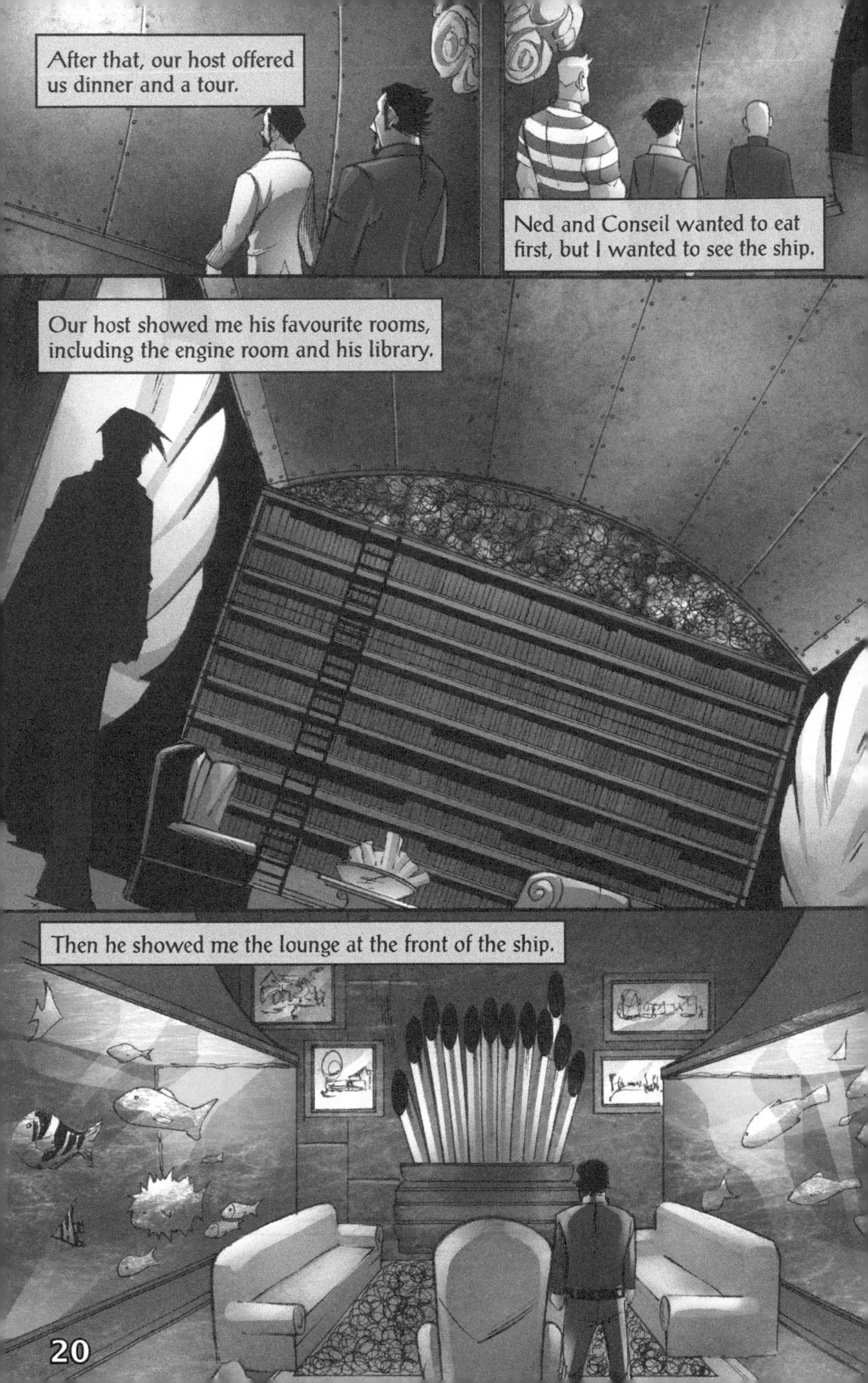
After that, our host offered us dinner and a tour.
Ned and Conseil wanted to eat first, but I wanted to see the ship.
Our host showed me his favourite rooms, including the engine room and his library.
Then he showed me the lounge at the front of the ship.

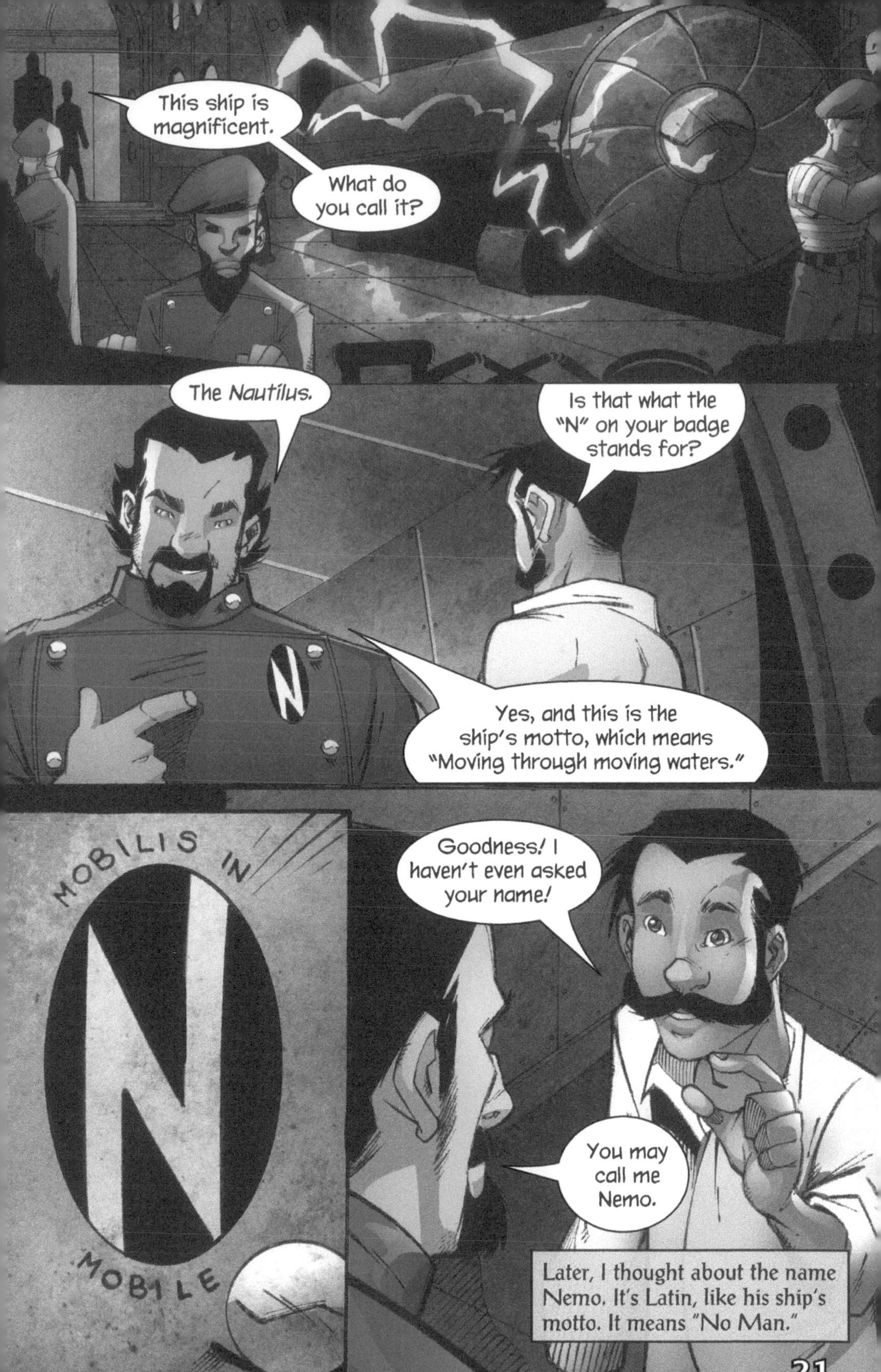
This ship is magnificent.
What do you call it?
The Nautilus.
Is that what the "N" on your badge stands for?
Yes, and this is the ship's motto, which means "Moving through moving waters."
MOBILIS IN MOBILE
Goodness! I haven't even asked your name!
You may call me Nemo.
Later, I thought about the name Nemo. It's Latin, like his ship's motto. It means "No Man."

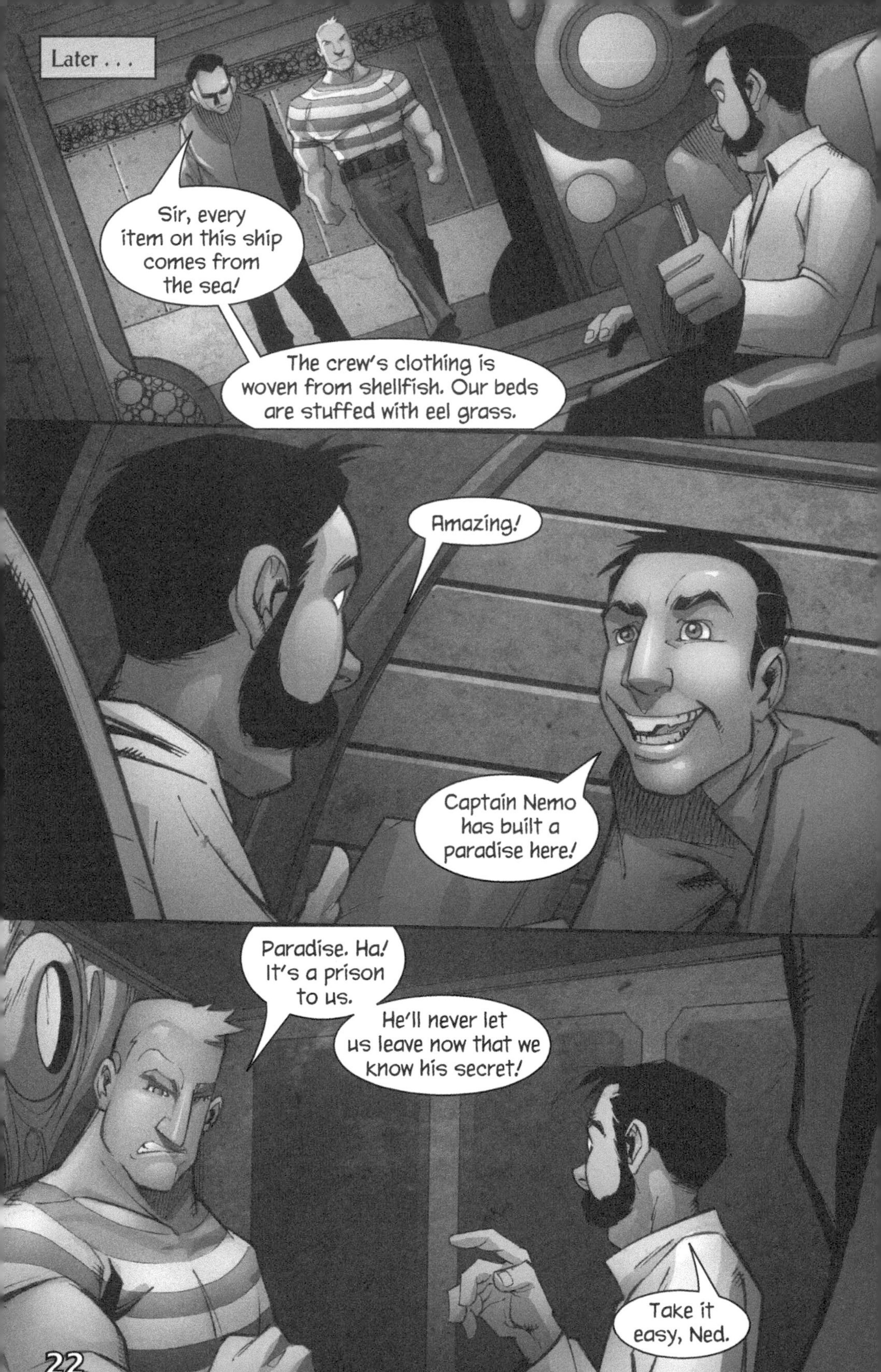
Later . . .
Sir, every item on this ship comes from the sea!
The crew's clothing is woven from shellfish. Our beds are stuffed with eel grass.
Amazing!
Captain Nemo has built a paradise here!
Paradise. Ha! It's a prison to us.
He'll never let us leave now that we know his secret!
Take it easy, Ned.

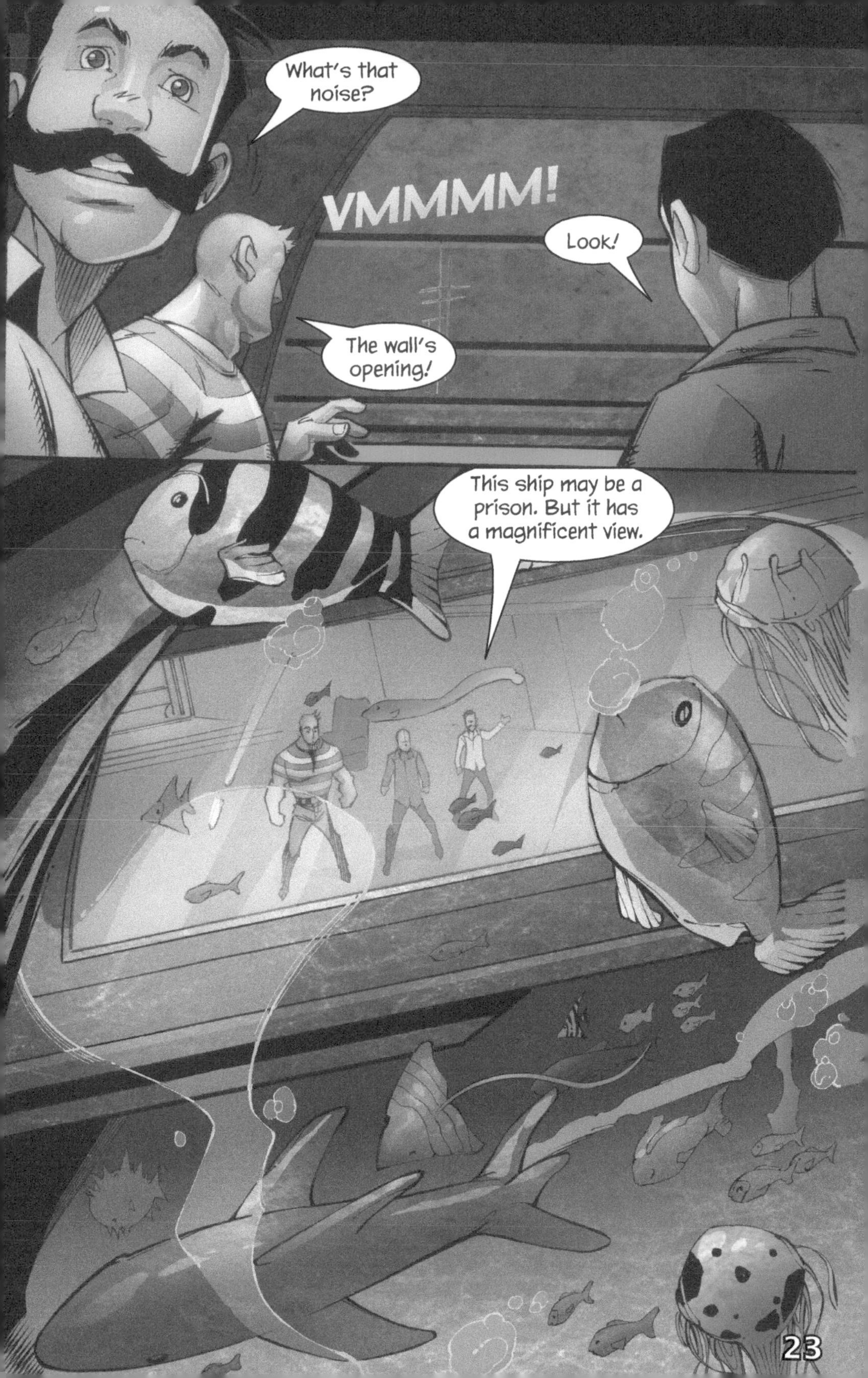
What's that noise?
VMMMM!
Look!
The wall's opening!
This ship may be a prison. But it has a magnificent view.

CHAPTER 3 : Death at Sea

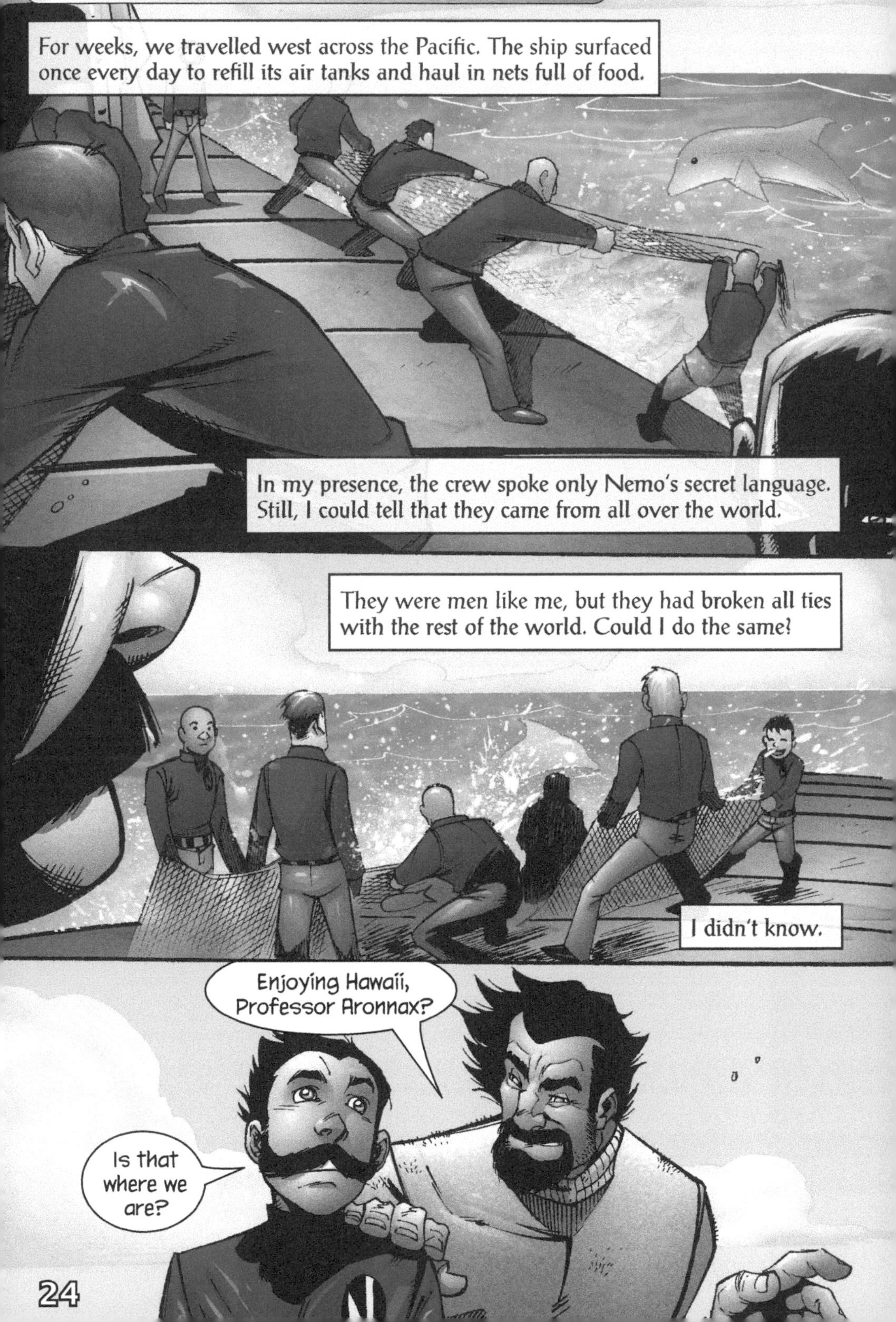
For weeks, we travelled west across the Pacific. The ship surfaced once every day to refill its air tanks and haul in nets full of food.
In my presence, the crew spoke only Nemo's secret language. Still, I could tell that they came from all over the world.
They were men like me, but they had broken all ties with the rest of the world. Could I do the same?
I didn't know.
Enjoying Hawaii, Professor Aronnax?
Is that where we are?

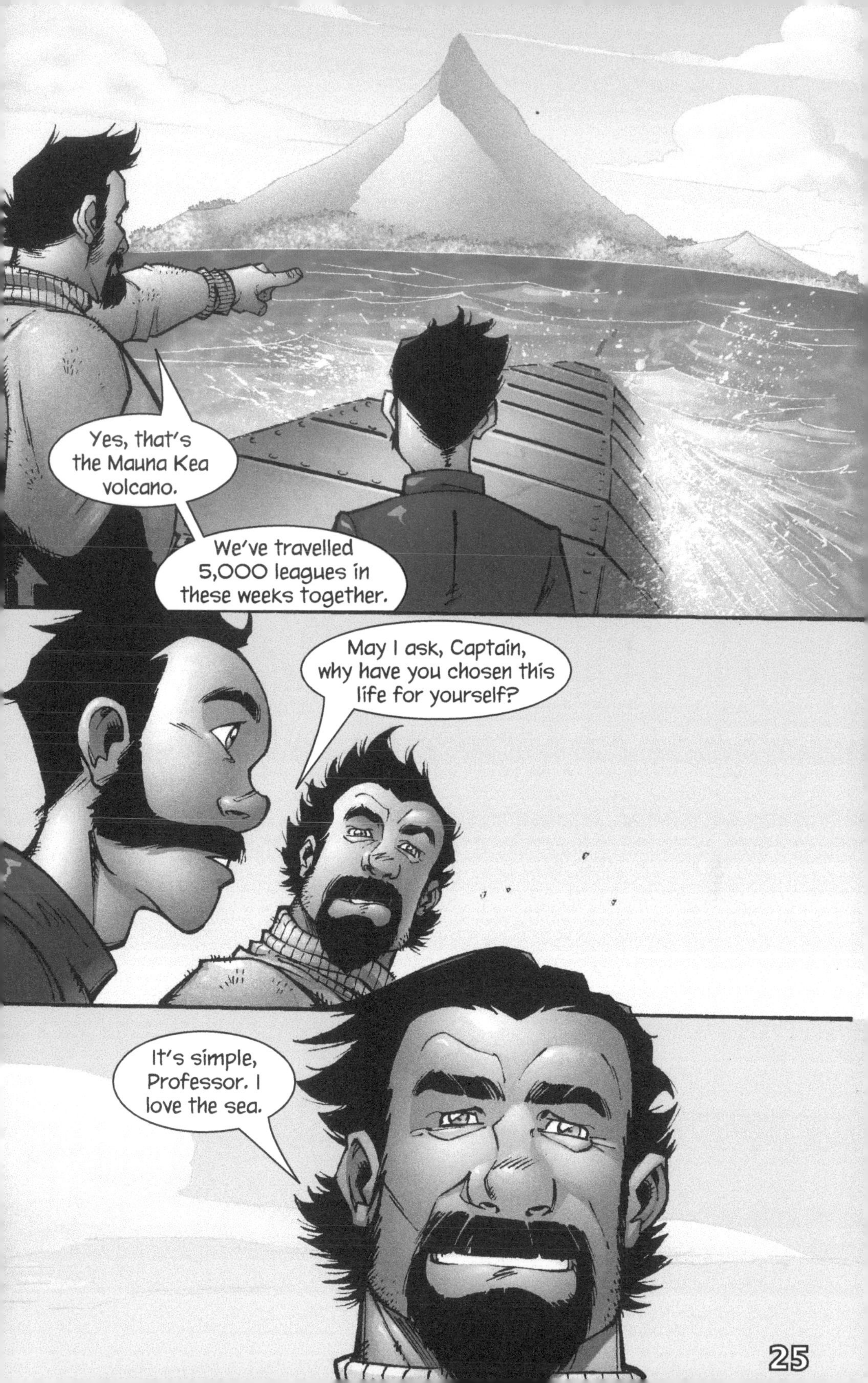
Yes, that's the Mauna Kea volcano.
We've travelled 5,000 leagues in these weeks together.
May I ask, Captain, why have you chosen this life for yourself?
It's simple, Professor. I love the sea.

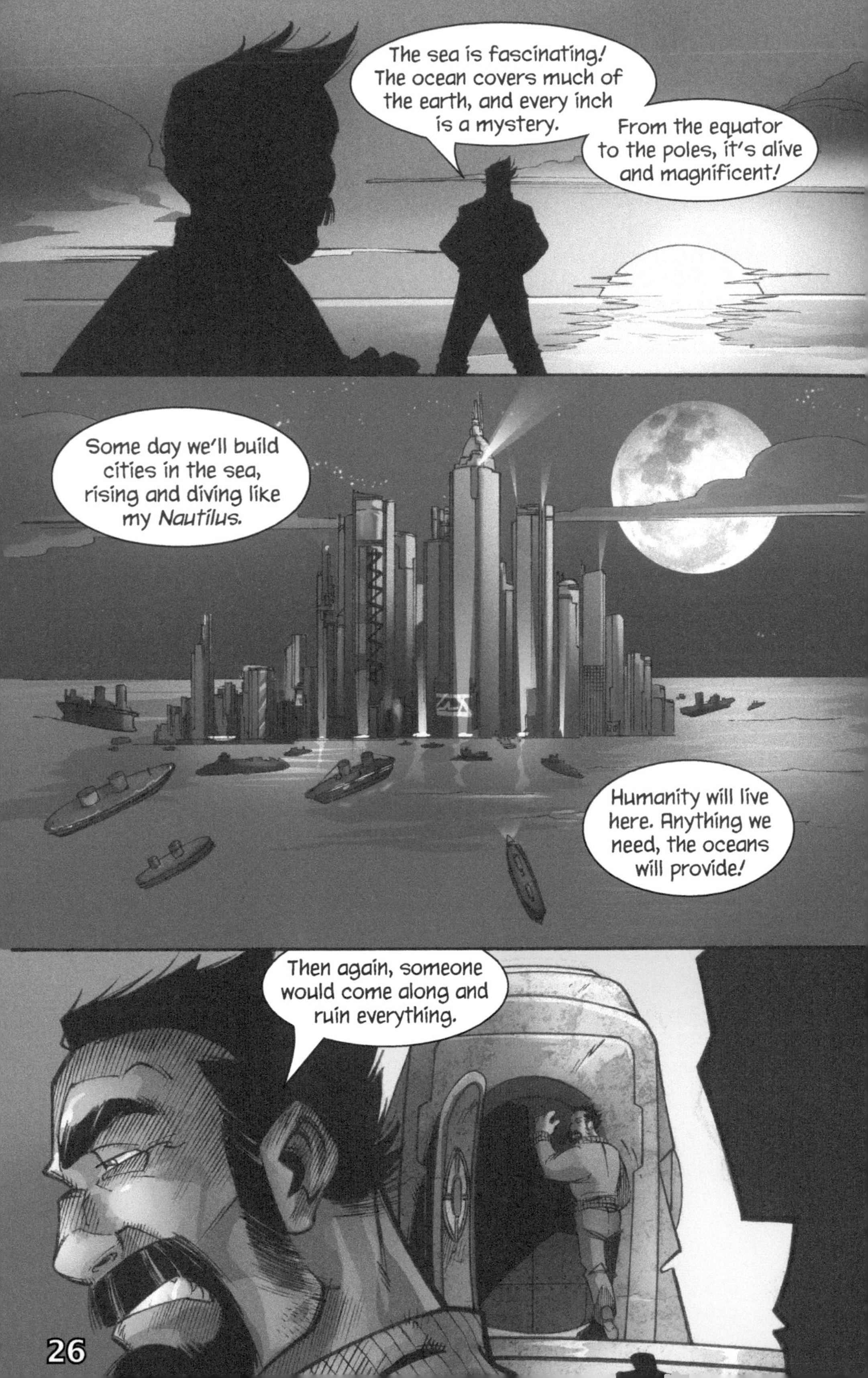
The sea is fascinating! The ocean covers much of the earth, and every inch is a mystery.
From the equator to the poles, it's alive and magnificent!
Some day we'll build cities in the sea, rising and diving like my *Nautilus*.
Humanity will live here. Anything we need, the oceans will provide!
Then again, someone would come along and ruin everything.

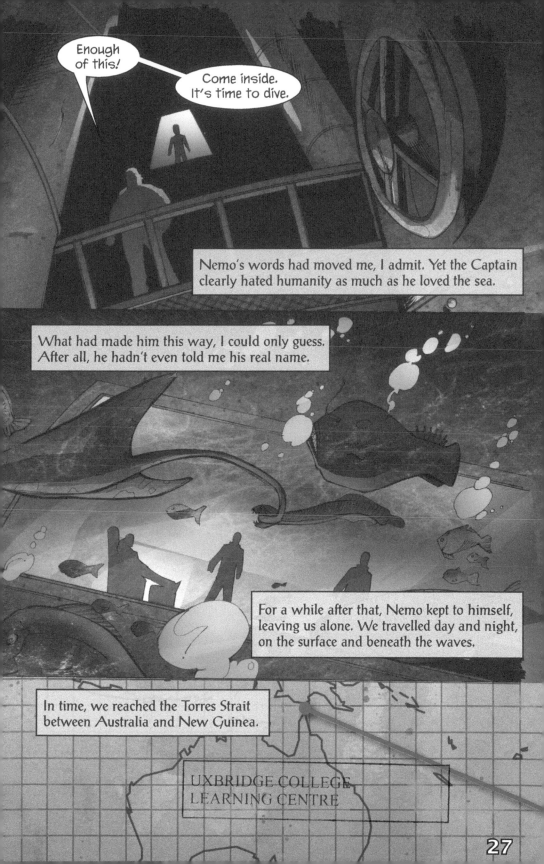

Enough of this!

Come inside. It's time to dive.

Nemo's words had moved me, I admit. Yet the Captain clearly hated humanity as much as he loved the sea.

What had made him this way, I could only guess. After all, he hadn't even told me his real name.

For a while after that, Nemo kept to himself, leaving us alone. We travelled day and night, on the surface and beneath the waves.

In time, we reached the Torres Strait between Australia and New Guinea.

UXBRIDGE COLLEGE
LEARNING CENTRE

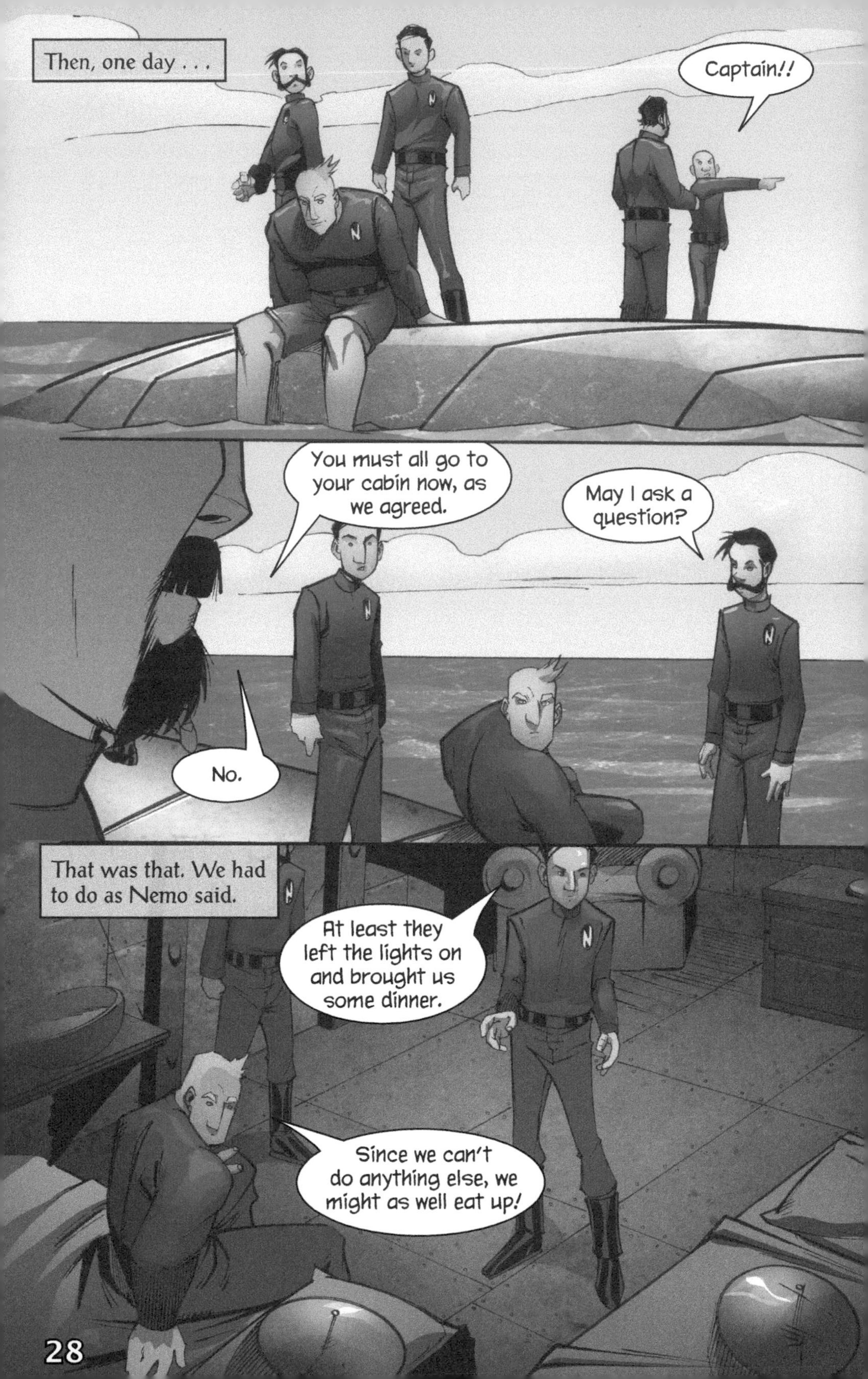

Then, one day . . .
Captain!!
You must all go to your cabin now, as we agreed.
May I ask a question?
No.
That was that. We had to do as Nemo said.
At least they left the lights on and brought us some dinner.
Since we can't do anything else, we might as well eat up!

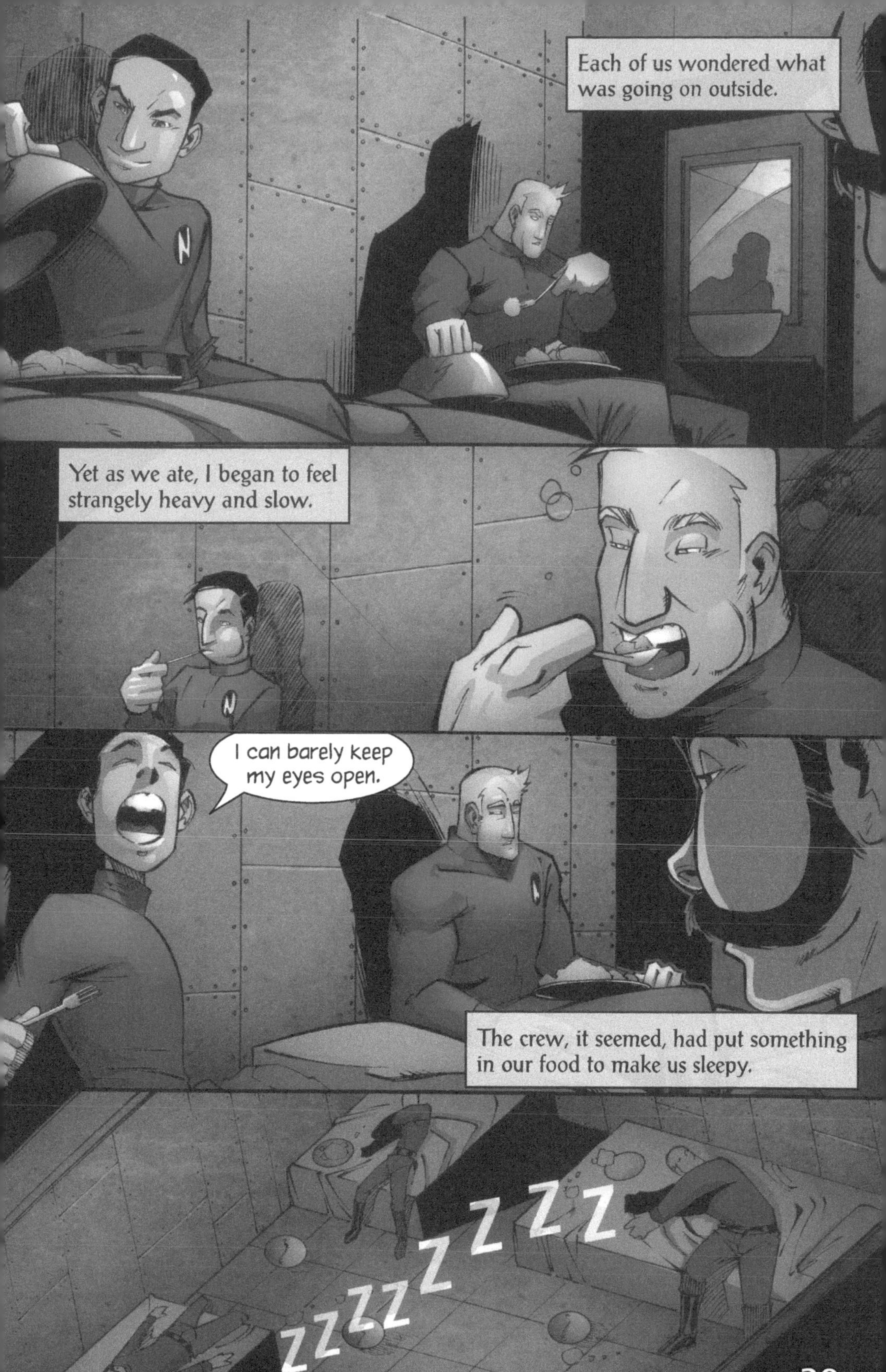
Each of us wondered what was going on outside.
Yet as we ate, I began to feel strangely heavy and slow.
I can barely keep my eyes open.
The crew, it seemed, had put something in our food to make us sleepy.
ZZZZZZZZZZ

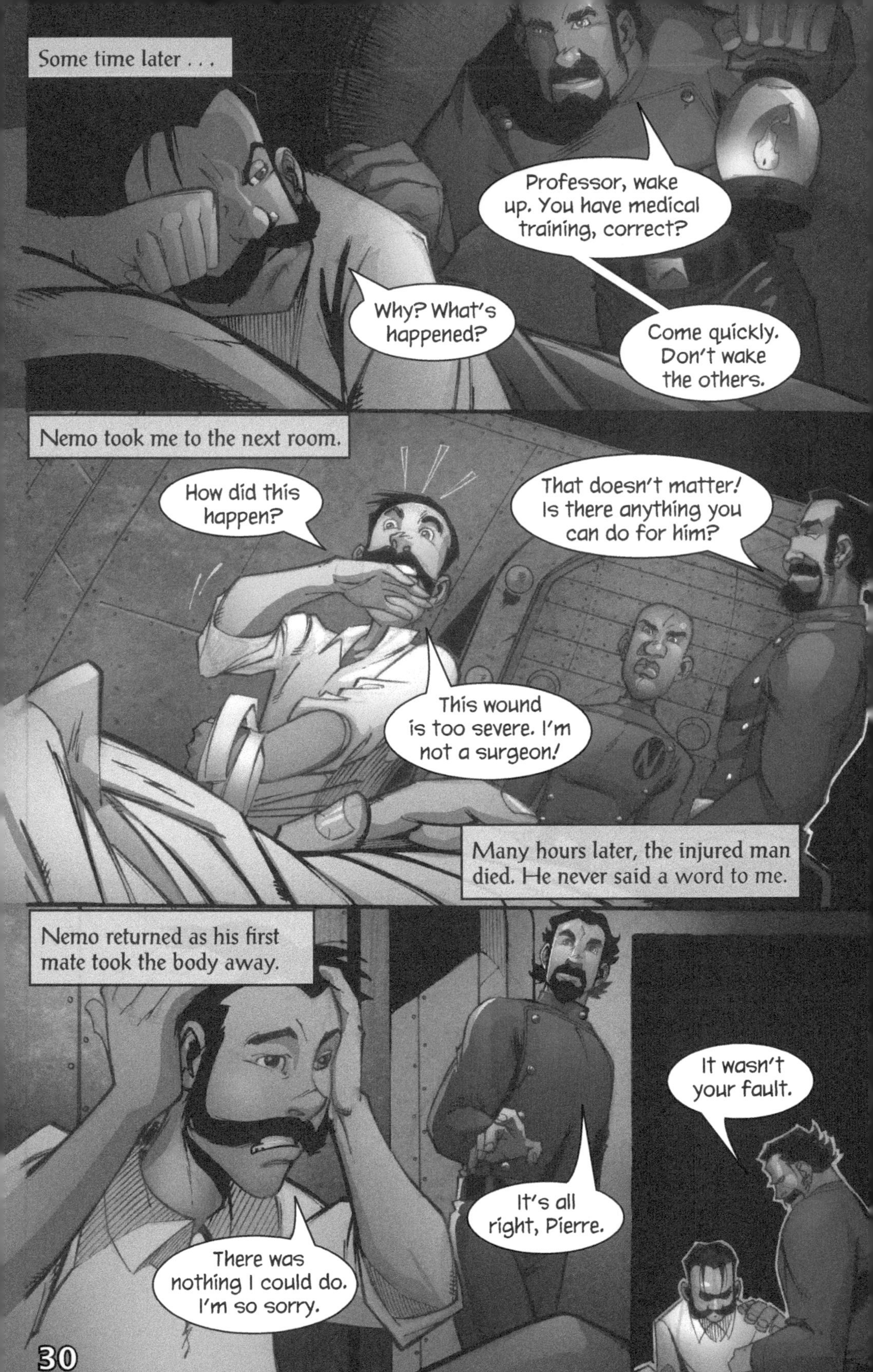

Some time later . . .
Professor, wake up. You have medical training, correct?
Why? What's happened?
Come quickly. Don't wake the others.
Nemo took me to the next room.
How did this happen?
That doesn't matter! Is there anything you can do for him?
This wound is too severe. I'm not a surgeon!
Many hours later, the injured man died. He never said a word to me.
Nemo returned as his first mate took the body away.
It wasn't your fault.
It's all right, Pierre.
There was nothing I could do. I'm so sorry.

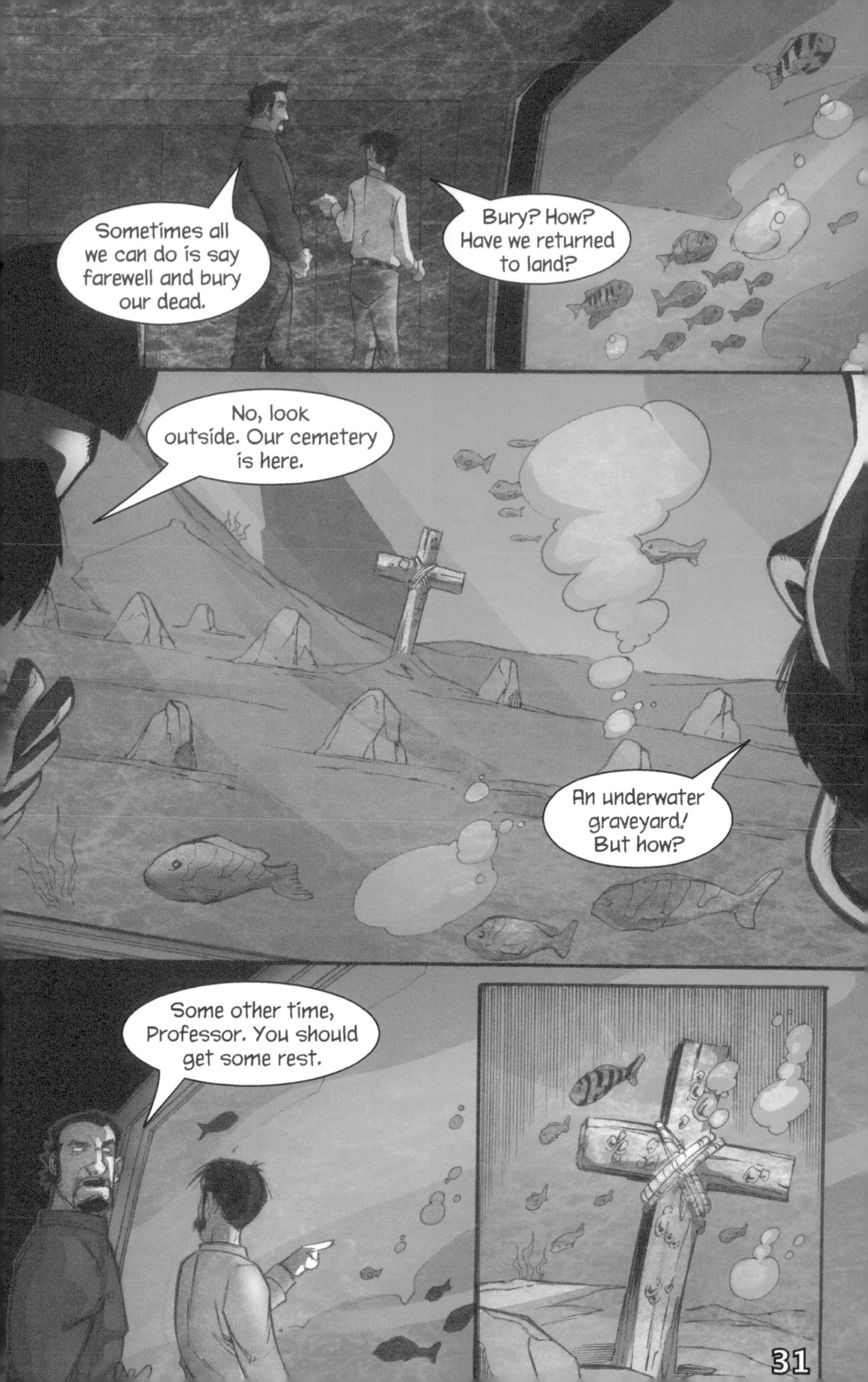
Sometimes all we can do is say farewell and bury our dead.
Bury? How? Have we returned to land?
No, look outside. Our cemetery is here.
An underwater graveyard! But how?
Some other time, Professor. You should get some rest.

CHAPTER 4 : Underwater Adventures

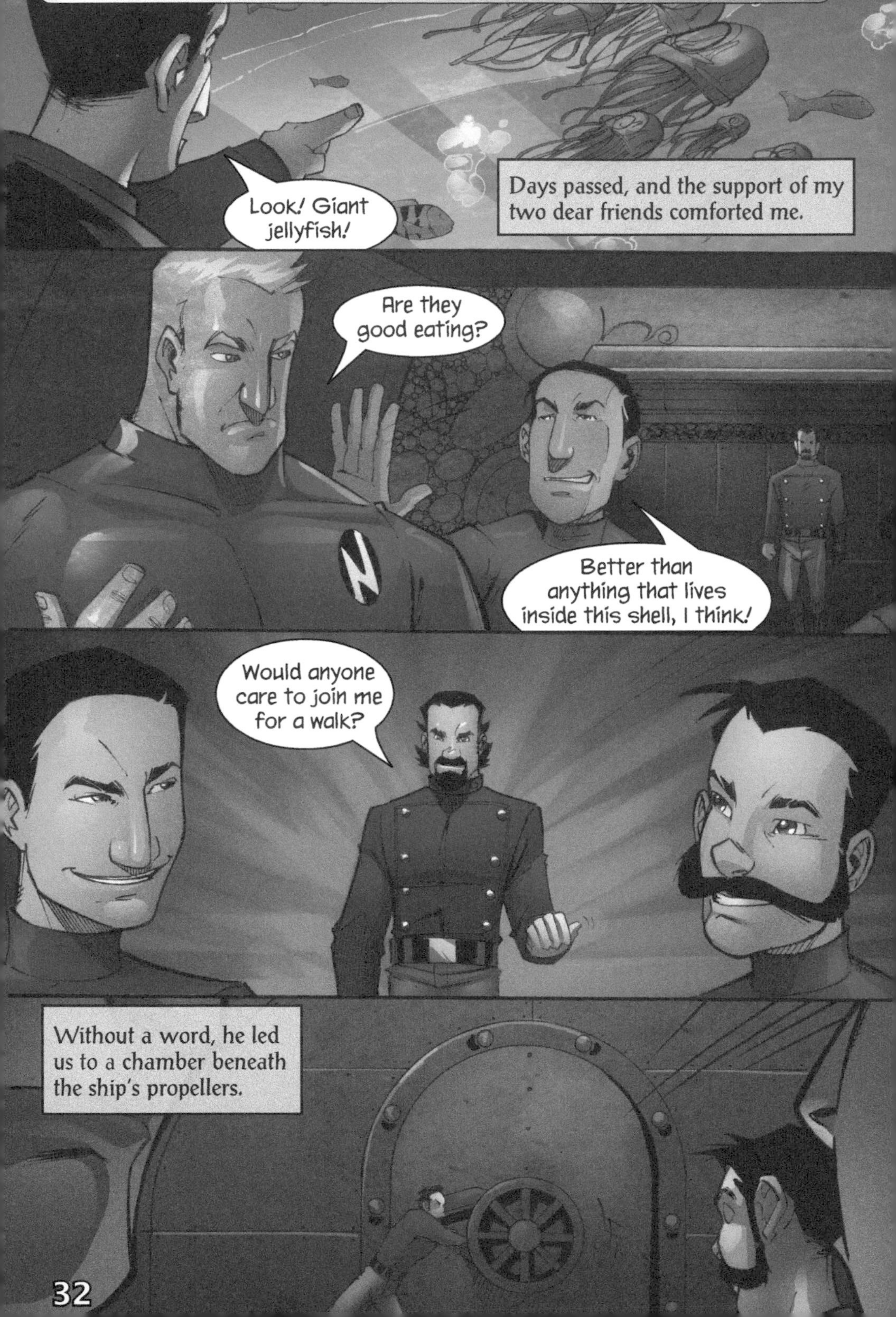
Look! Giant jellyfish!
Days passed, and the support of my two dear friends comforted me.
Are they good eating?
Better than anything that lives inside this shell, I think!
Would anyone care to join me for a walk?
Without a word, he led us to a chamber beneath the ship's propellers.

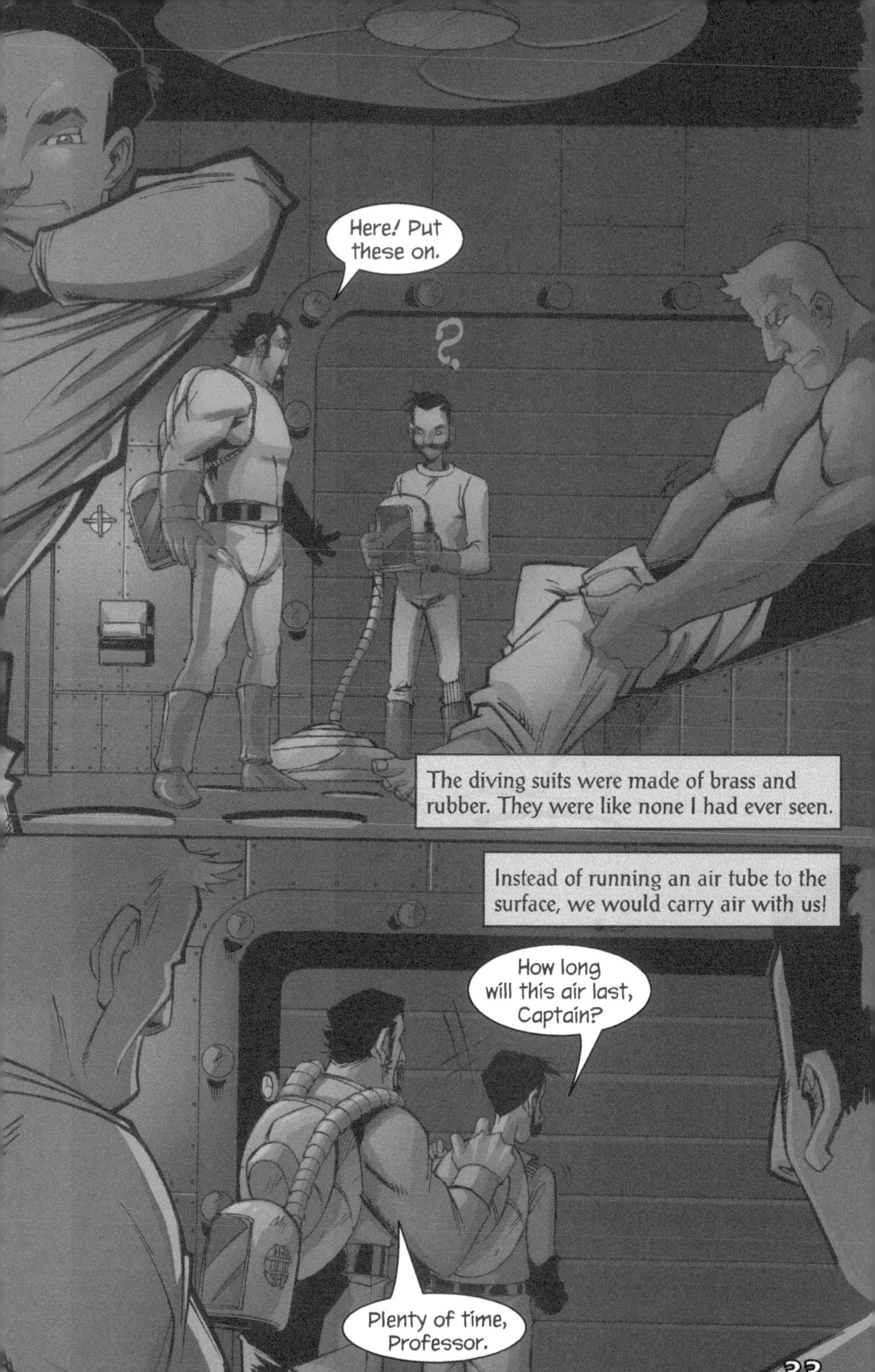
Here! Put these on.
?
The diving suits were made of brass and rubber. They were like none I had ever seen.
Instead of running an air tube to the surface, we would carry air with us!
How long will this air last, Captain?
Plenty of time, Professor.

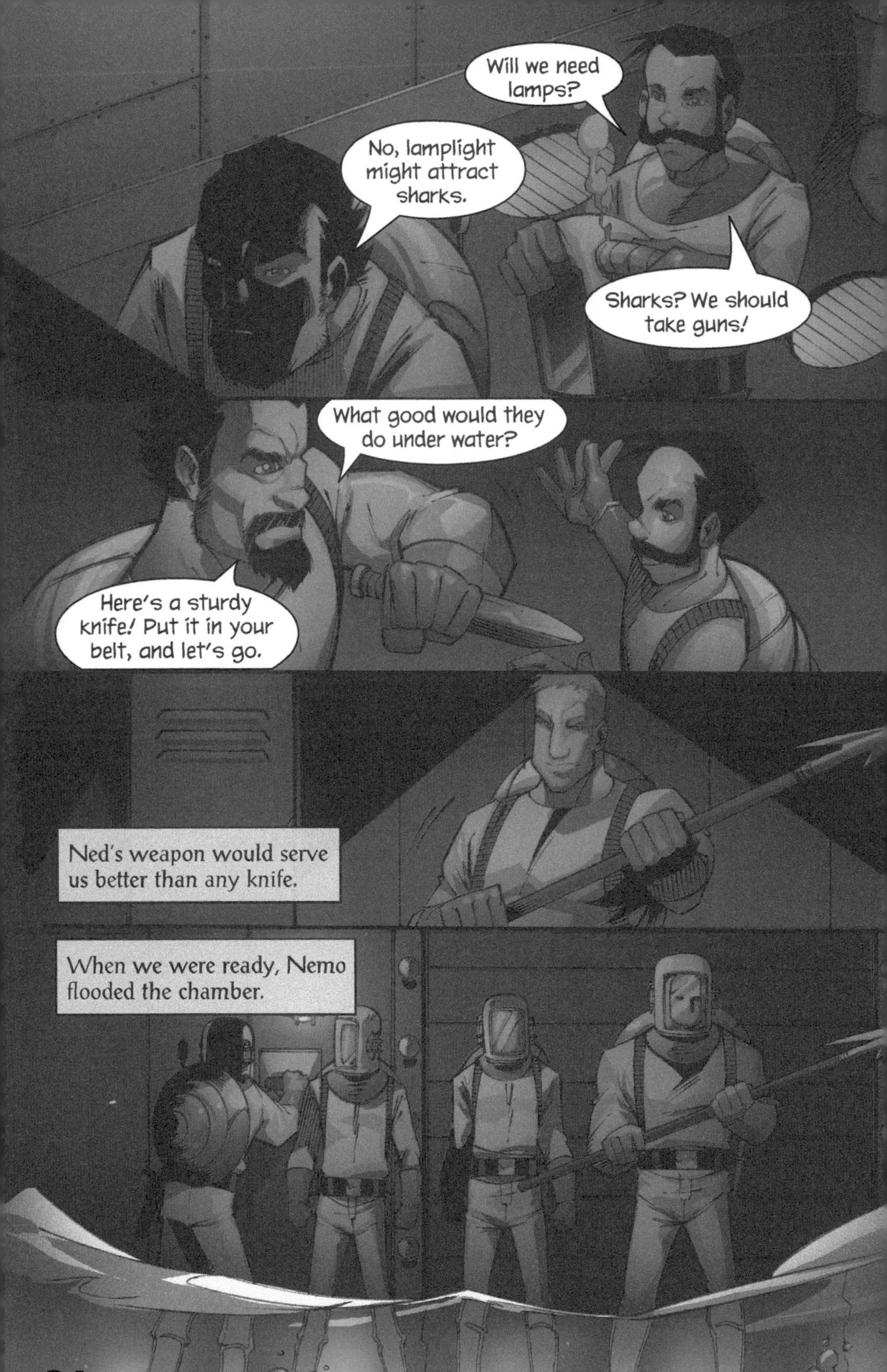
Will we need lamps?
No, lamplight might attract sharks.
Sharks? We should take guns!
What good would they do under water?
Here's a sturdy knife! Put it in your belt, and let's go.
Ned's weapon would serve us better than any knife.
When we were ready, Nemo flooded the chamber.

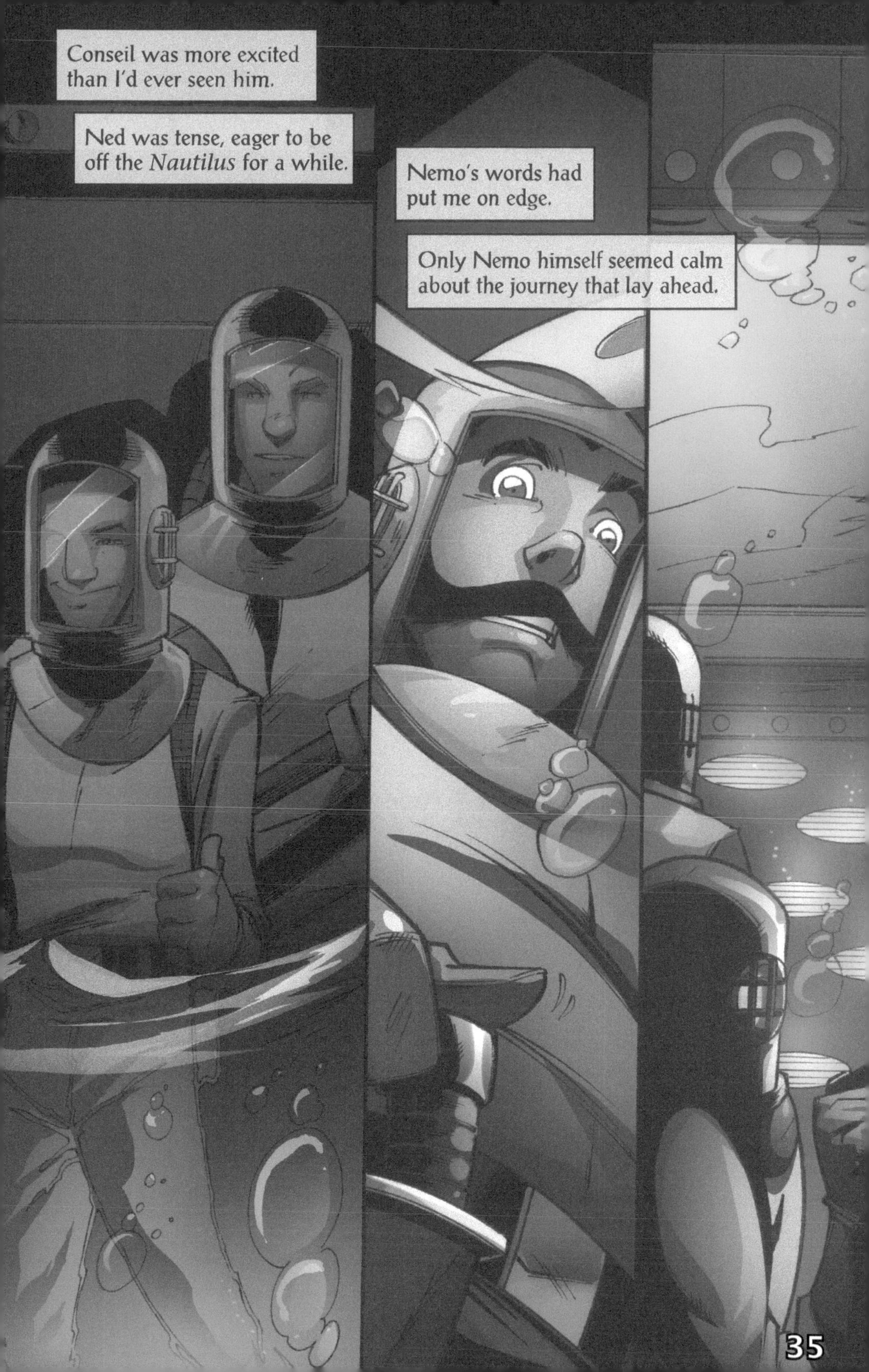
Conseil was more excited than I'd ever seen him.
Ned was tense, eager to be off the *Nautilus* for a while.
Nemo's words had put me on edge.
Only Nemo himself seemed calm about the journey that lay ahead.

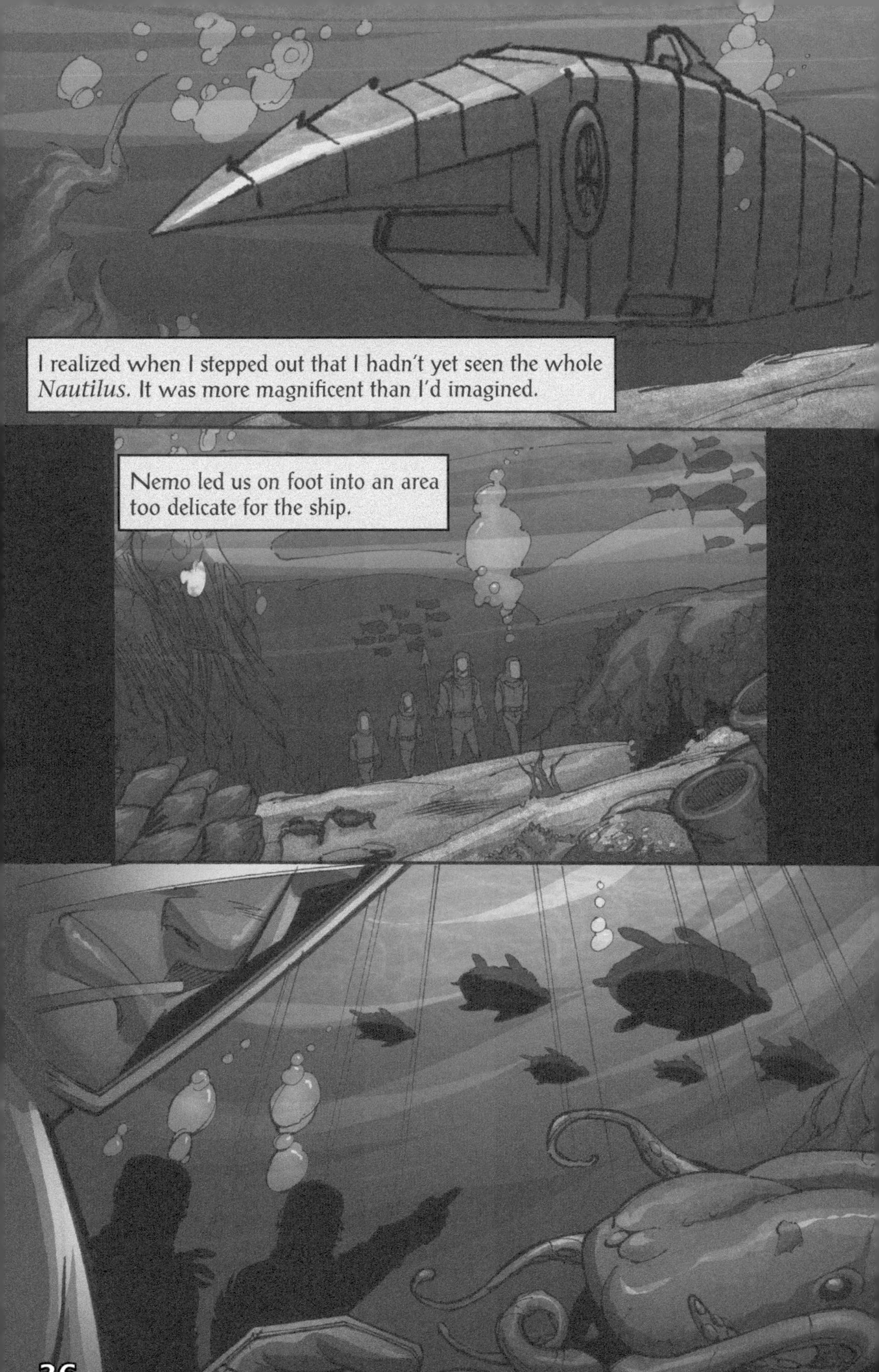
I realized when I stepped out that I hadn't yet seen the whole *Nautilus*. It was more magnificent than I'd imagined.
Nemo led us on foot into an area too delicate for the ship.

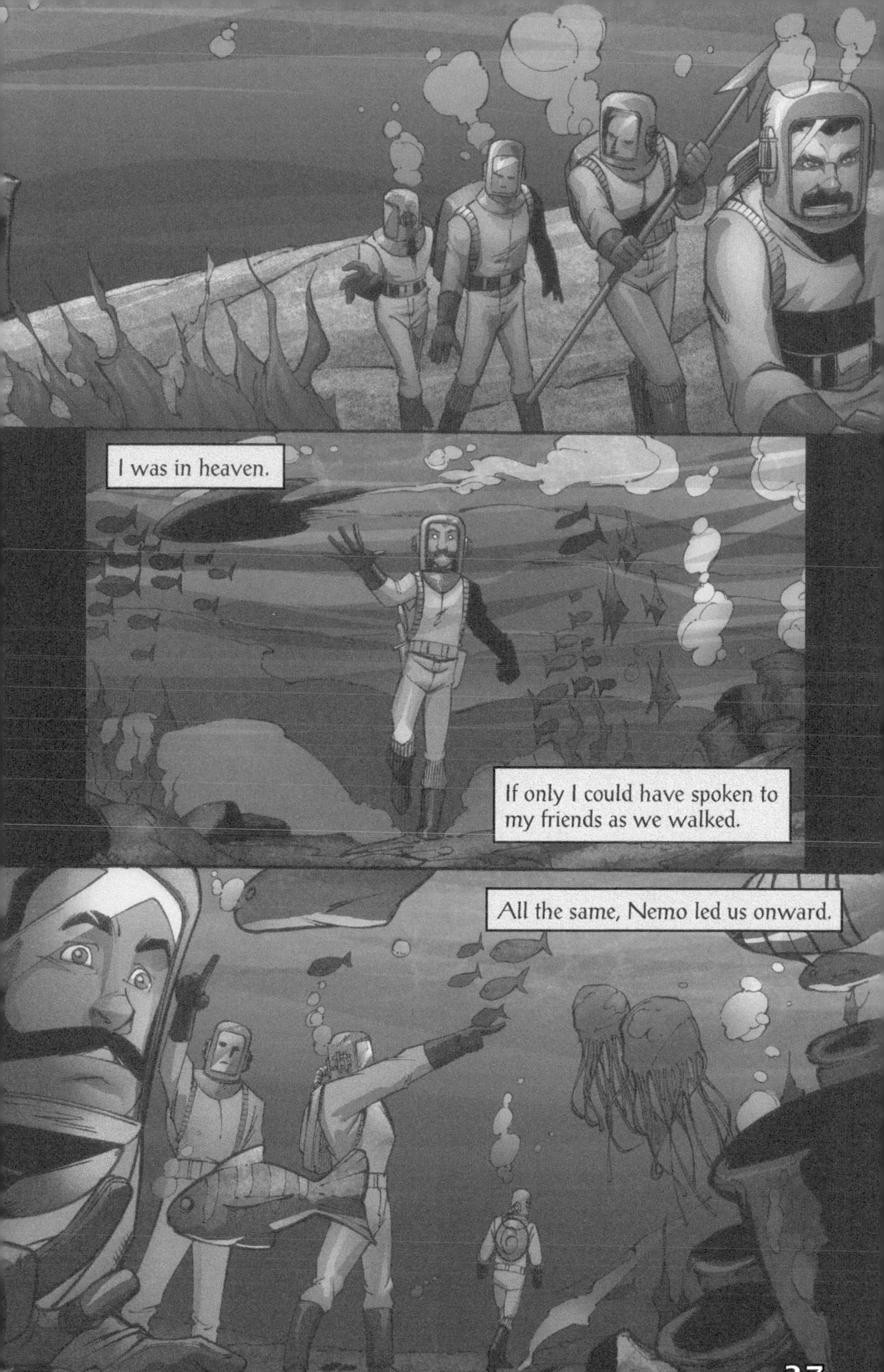
I was in heaven.
If only I could have spoken to my friends as we walked.
All the same, Nemo led us onward.

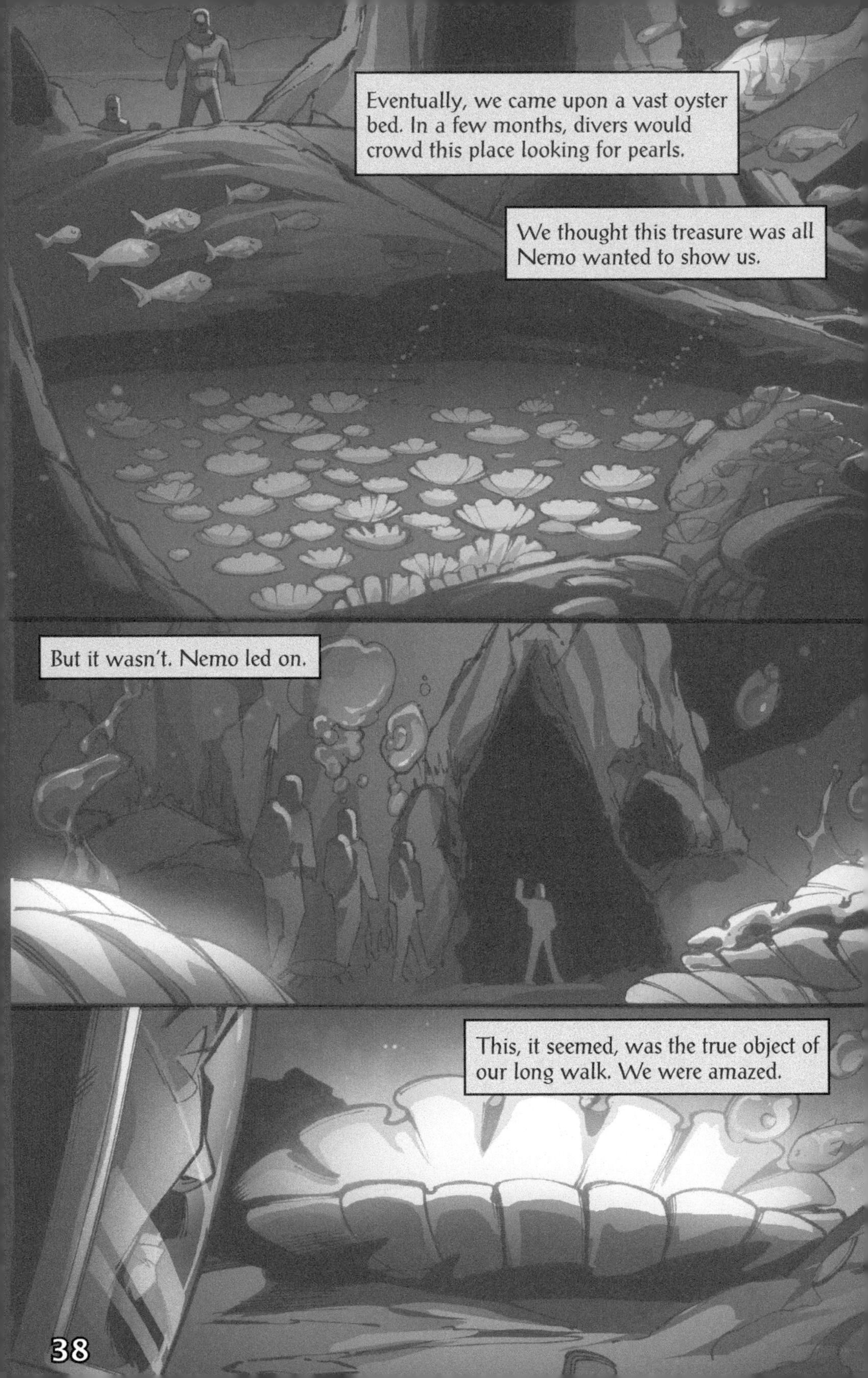
Eventually, we came upon a vast oyster bed. In a few months, divers would crowd this place looking for pearls.
We thought this treasure was all Nemo wanted to show us.
But it wasn't. Nemo led on.
This, it seemed, was the true object of our long walk. We were amazed.

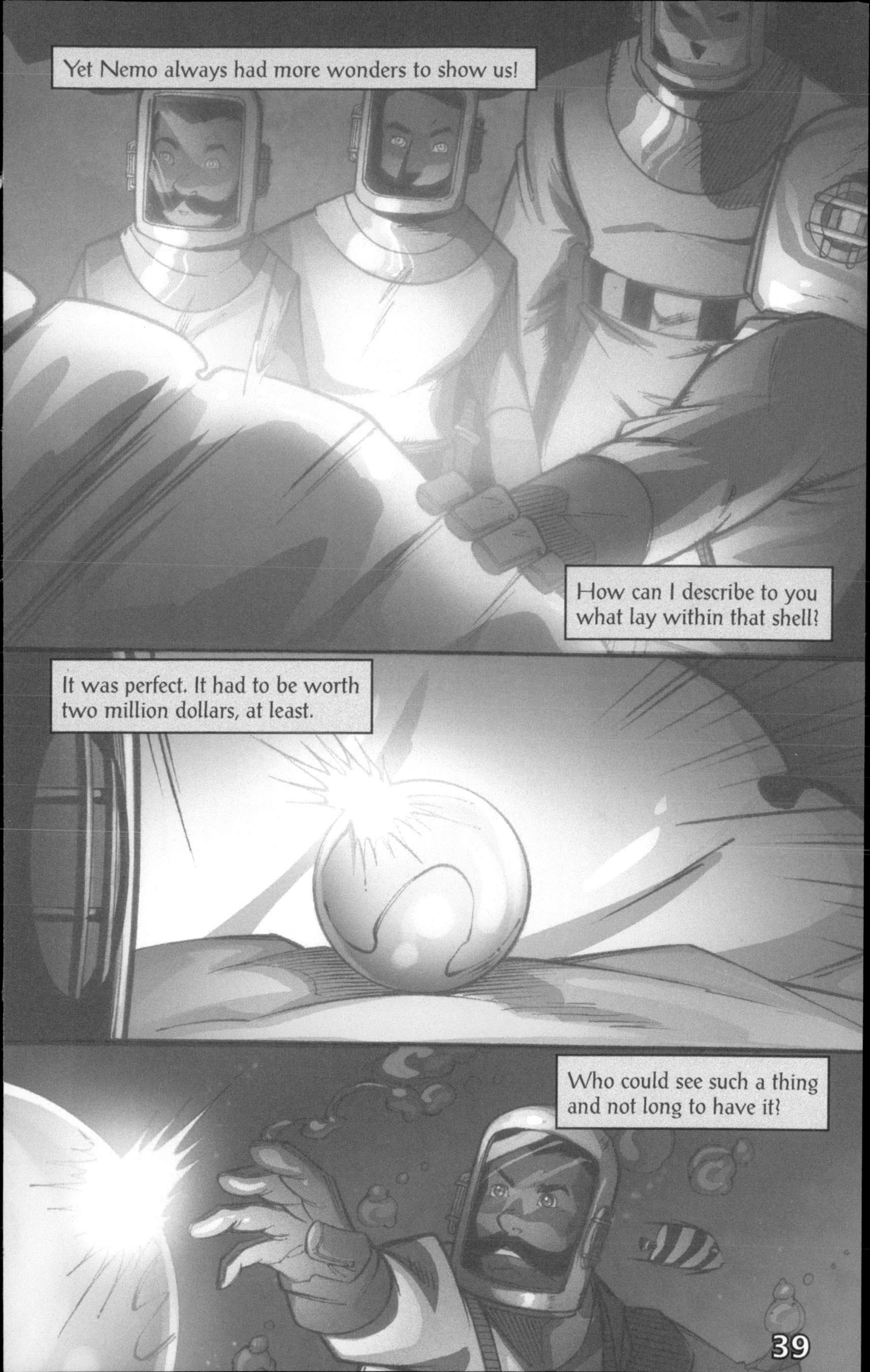
Yet Nemo always had more wonders to show us!
How can I describe to you what lay within that shell?
It was perfect. It had to be worth two million dollars, at least.
Who could see such a thing and not long to have it?

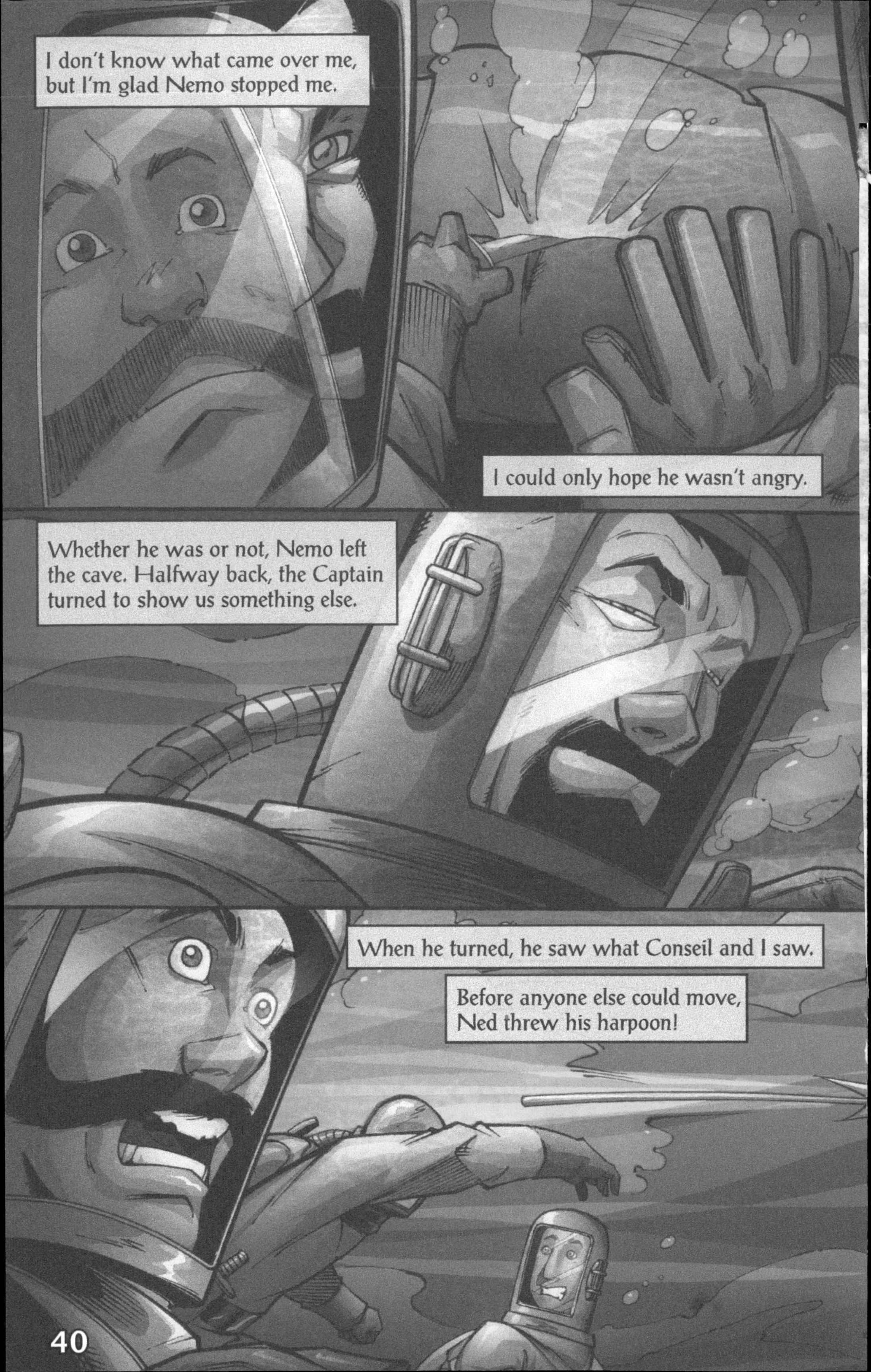
I don't know what came over me, but I'm glad Nemo stopped me.
I could only hope he wasn't angry.
Whether he was or not, Nemo left the cave. Halfway back, the Captain turned to show us something else.
When he turned, he saw what Conseil and I saw.
Before anyone else could move, Ned threw his harpoon!

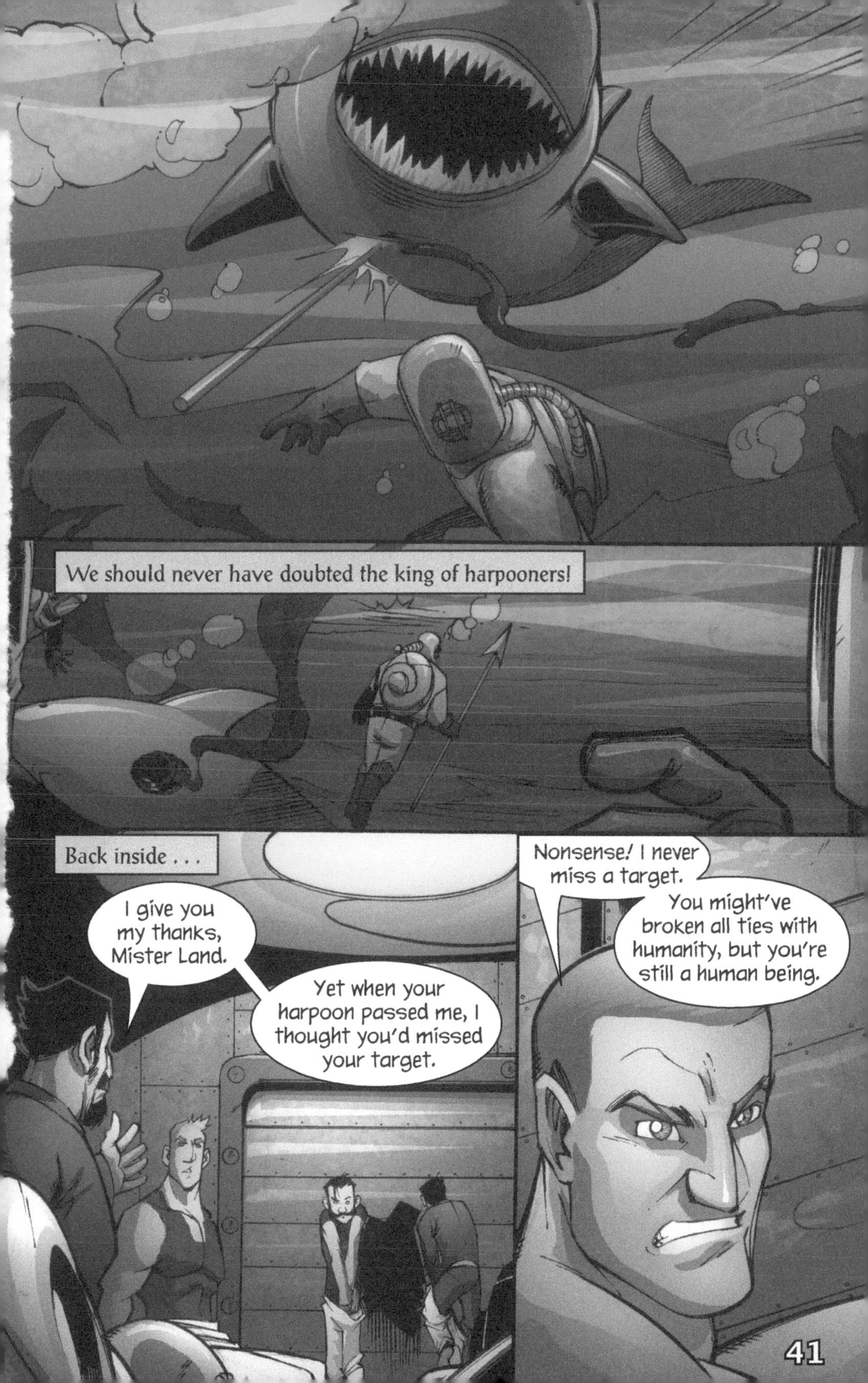
We should never have doubted the king of harpooners!
Back inside . . .
I give you my thanks, Mister Land.
Yet when your harpoon passed me, I thought you'd missed your target.
Nonsense! I never miss a target.
You might've broken all ties with humanity, but you're still a human being.

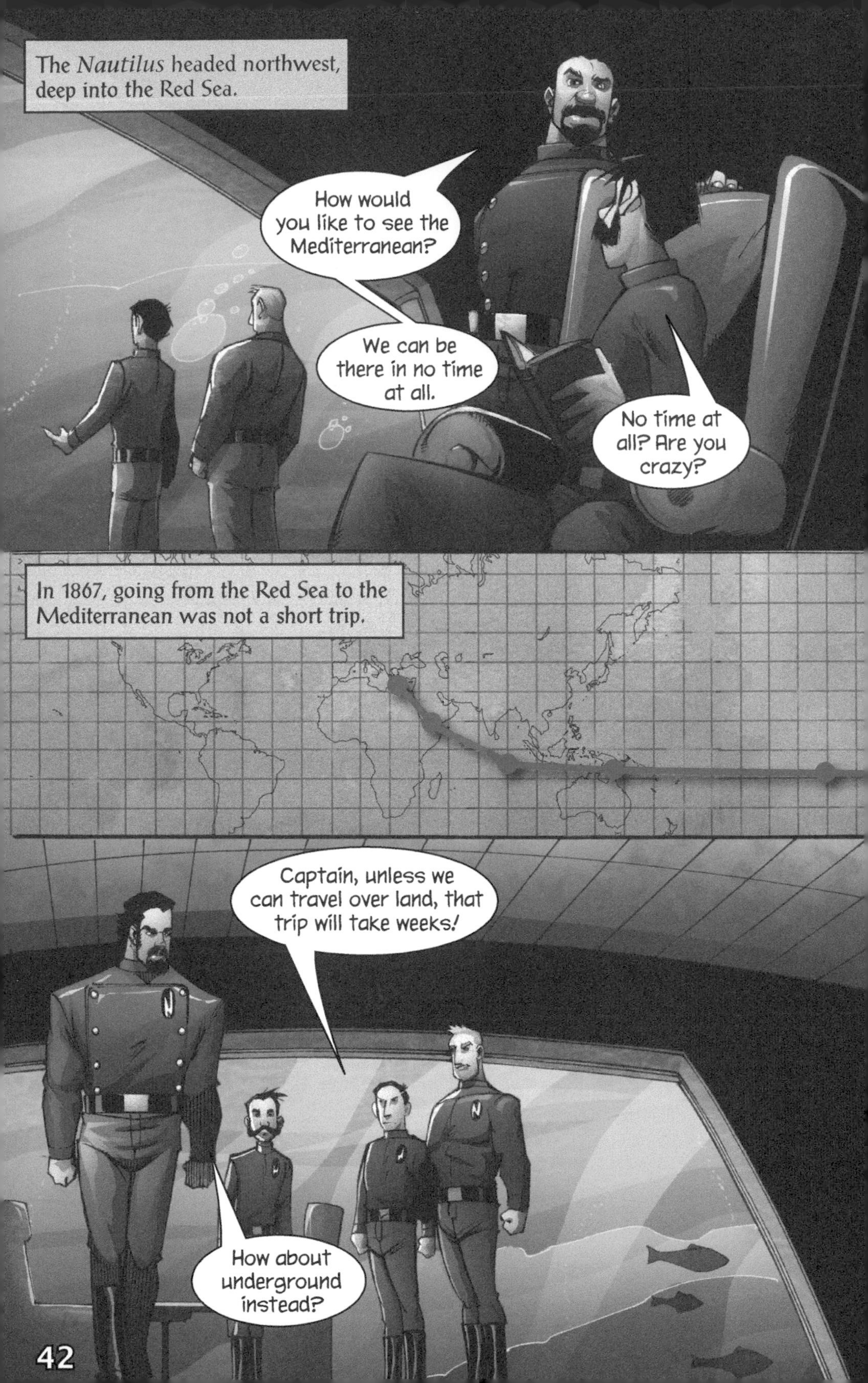
The *Nautilus* headed northwest, deep into the Red Sea.
How would you like to see the Mediterranean?
We can be there in no time at all.
No time at all? Are you crazy?
In 1867, going from the Red Sea to the Mediterranean was not a short trip.
Captain, unless we can travel over land, that trip will take weeks!
How about underground instead?

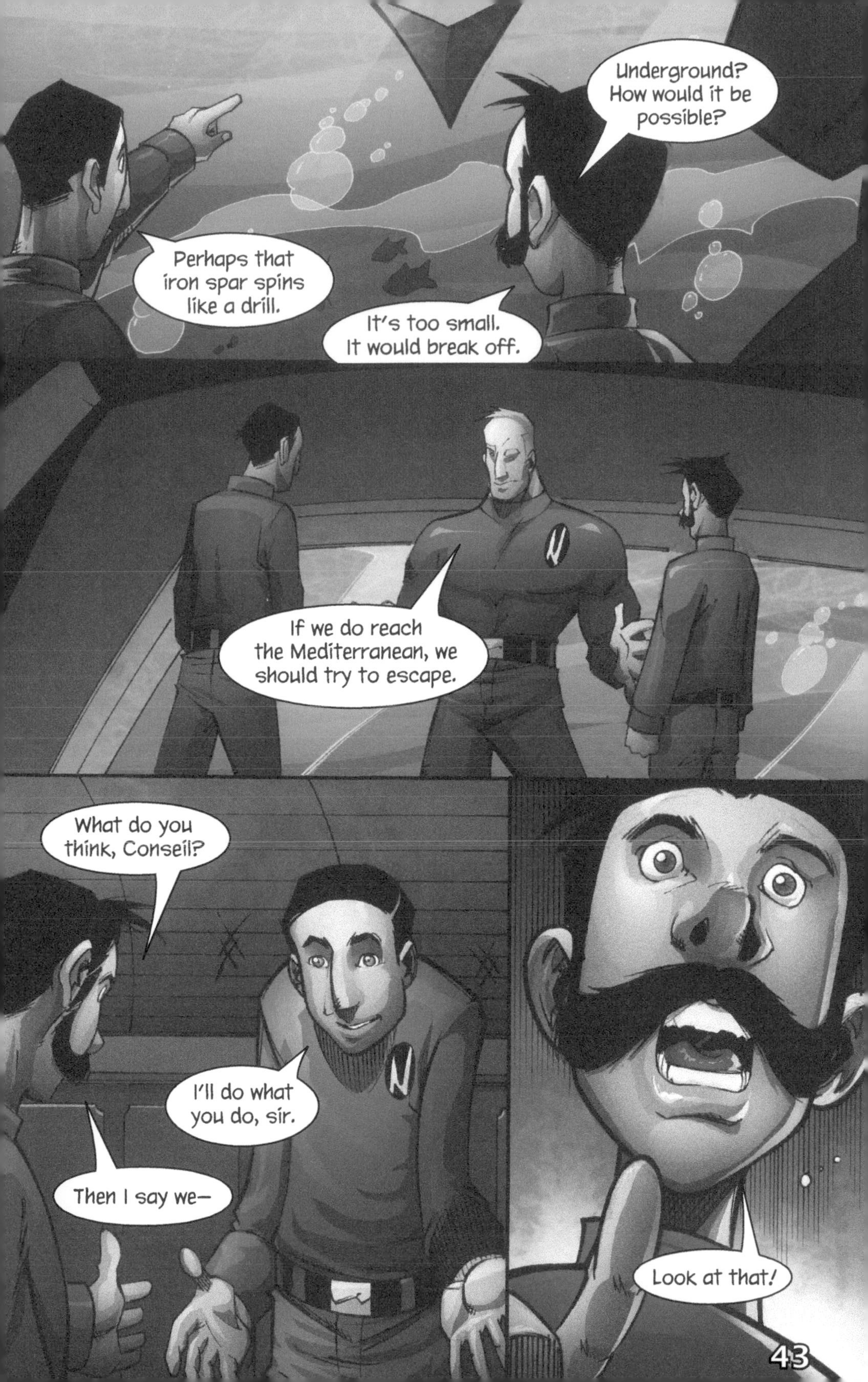
Underground? How would it be possible?
Perhaps that iron spar spins like a drill.
It's too small. It would break off.
If we do reach the Mediterranean, we should try to escape.
What do you think, Conseil?
I'll do what you do, sir.
Then I say we–
Look at that!

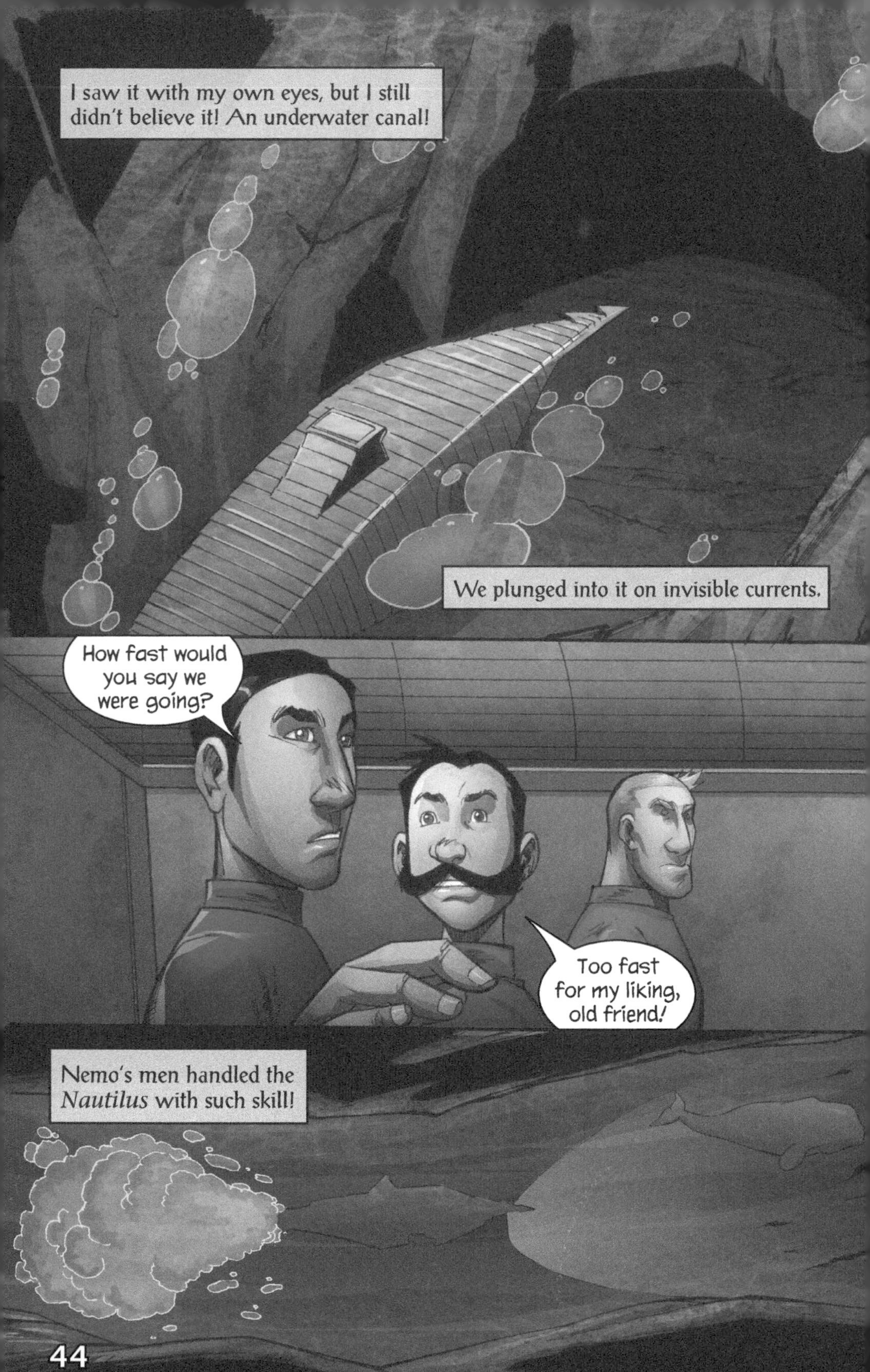
I saw it with my own eyes, but I still didn't believe it! An underwater canal!
We plunged into it on invisible currents.
How fast would you say we were going?
Too fast for my liking, old friend!
Nemo's men handled the *Nautilus* with such skill!

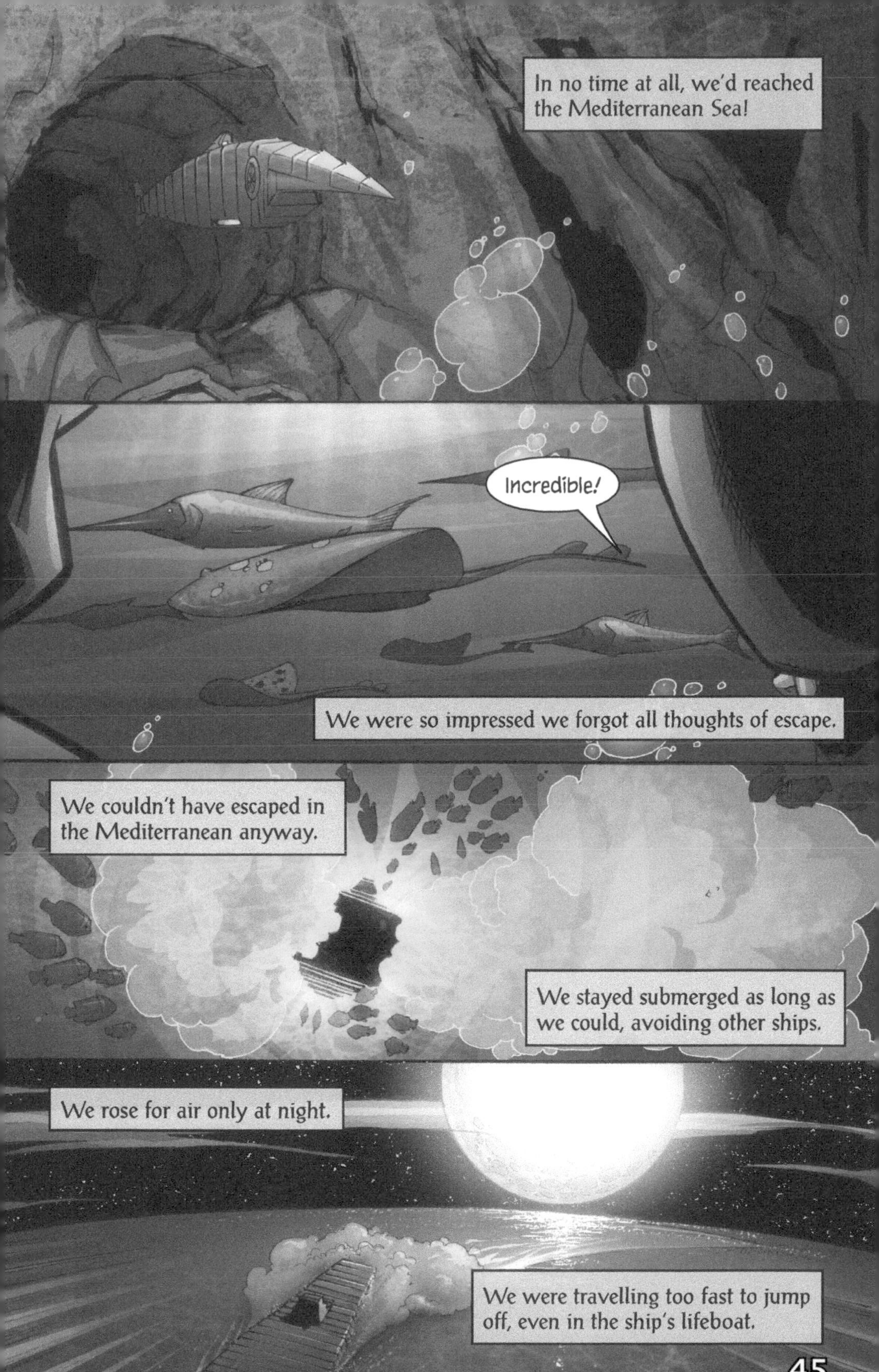
In no time at all, we'd reached the Mediterranean Sea!
Incredible!
We were so impressed we forgot all thoughts of escape.
We couldn't have escaped in the Mediterranean anyway.
We stayed submerged as long as we could, avoiding other ships.
We rose for air only at night.
We were travelling too fast to jump off, even in the ship's lifeboat.

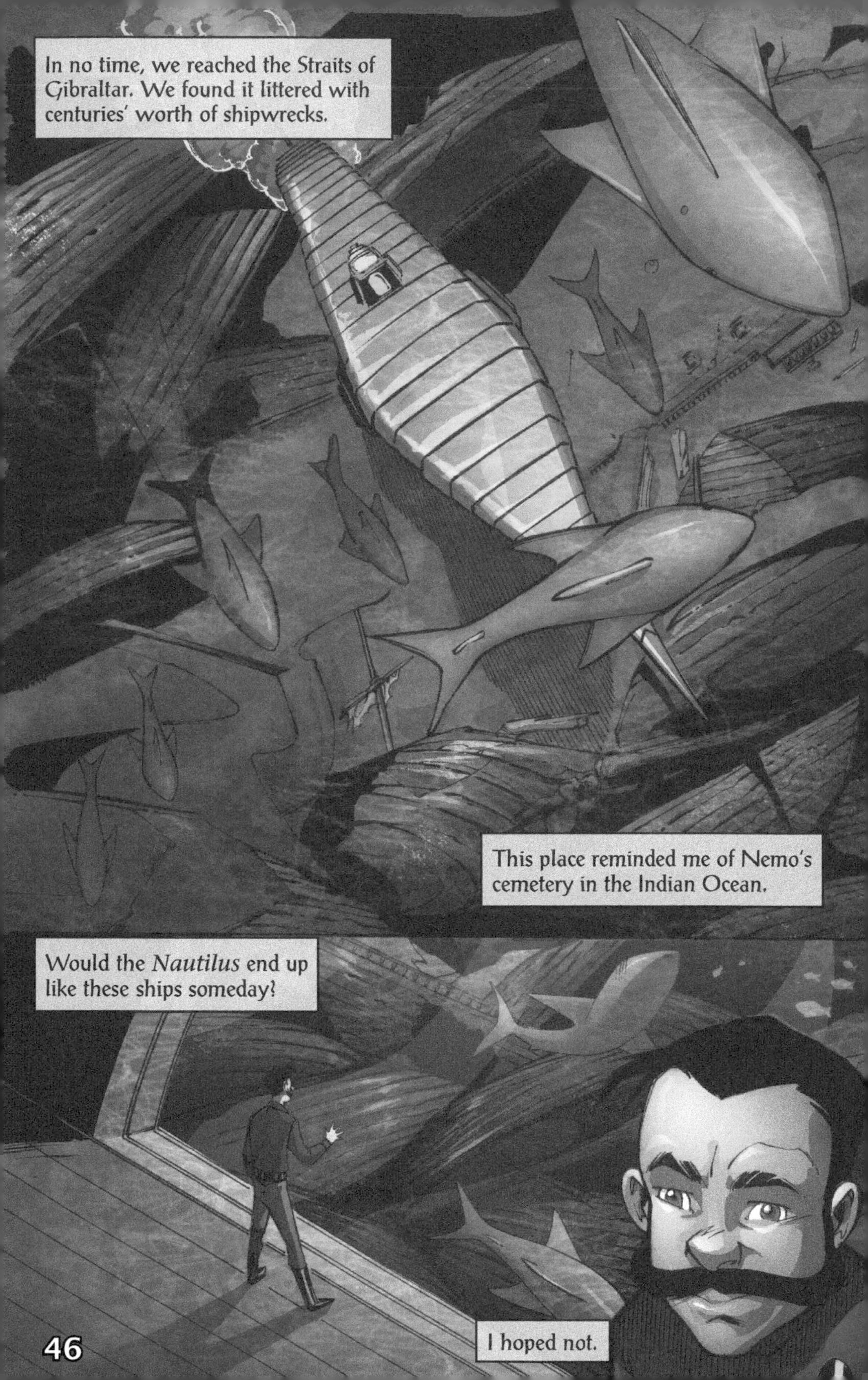

In no time, we reached the Straits of Gibraltar. We found it littered with centuries' worth of shipwrecks.
This place reminded me of Nemo's cemetery in the Indian Ocean.
Would the *Nautilus* end up like these ships someday?
I hoped not.

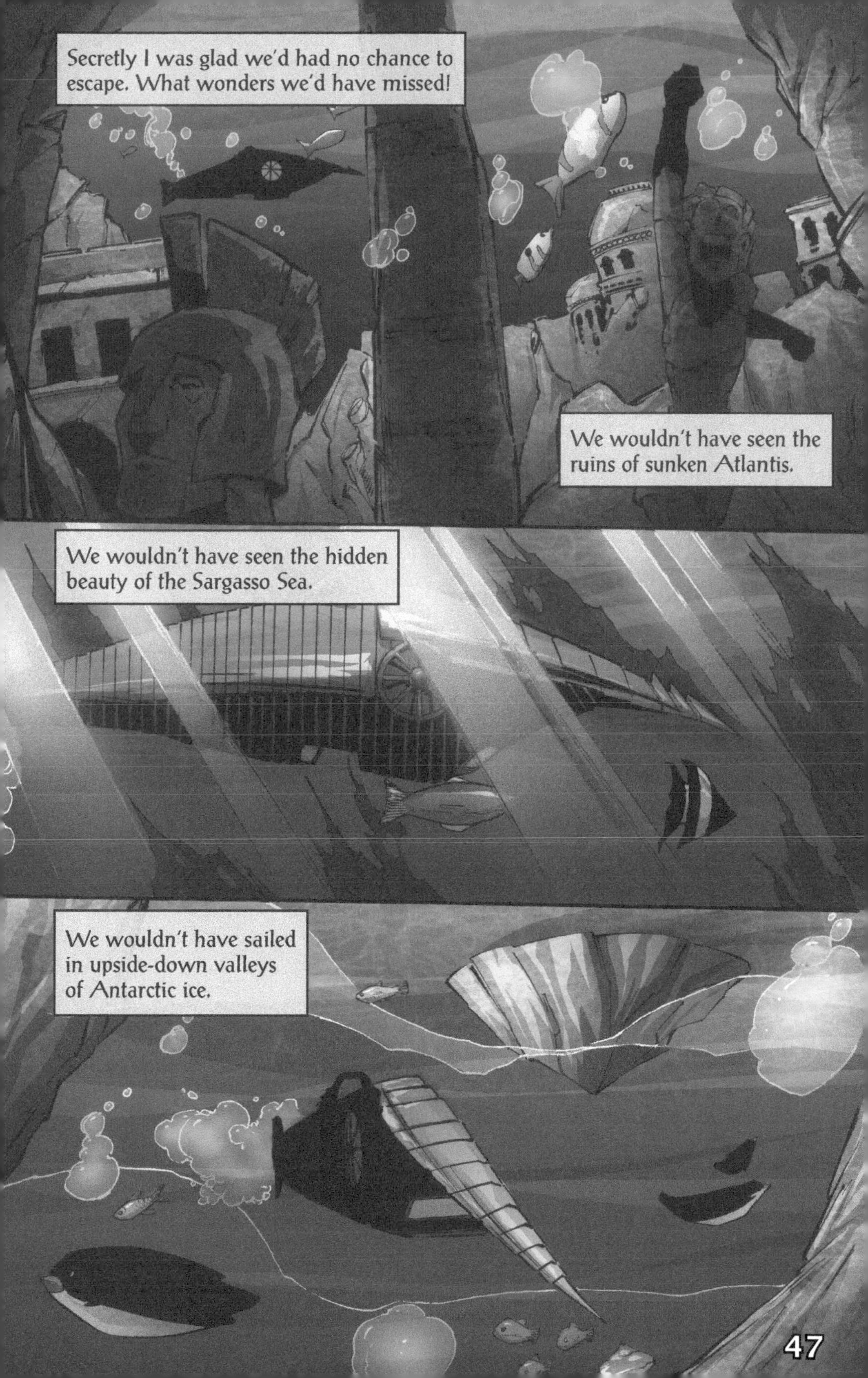
Secretly I was glad we'd had no chance to escape. What wonders we'd have missed!
We wouldn't have seen the ruins of sunken Atlantis.
We wouldn't have seen the hidden beauty of the Sargasso Sea.
We wouldn't have sailed in upside-down valleys of Antarctic ice.

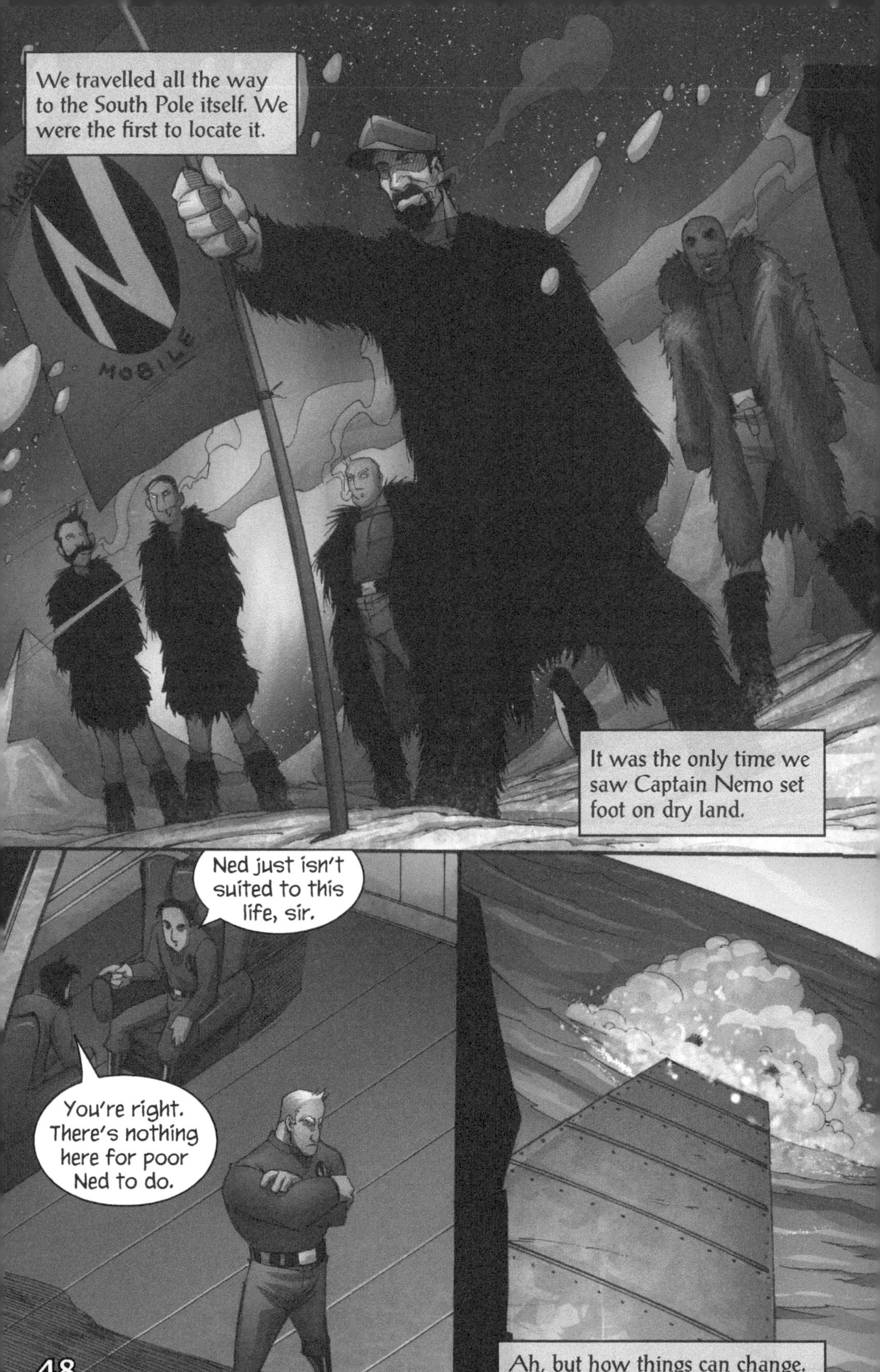
We travelled all the way to the South Pole itself. We were the first to locate it.
MOBILE
MOBILE
It was the only time we saw Captain Nemo set foot on dry land.
Ned just isn't suited to this life, sir.
You're right. There's nothing here for poor Ned to do.
Ah, but how things can change.

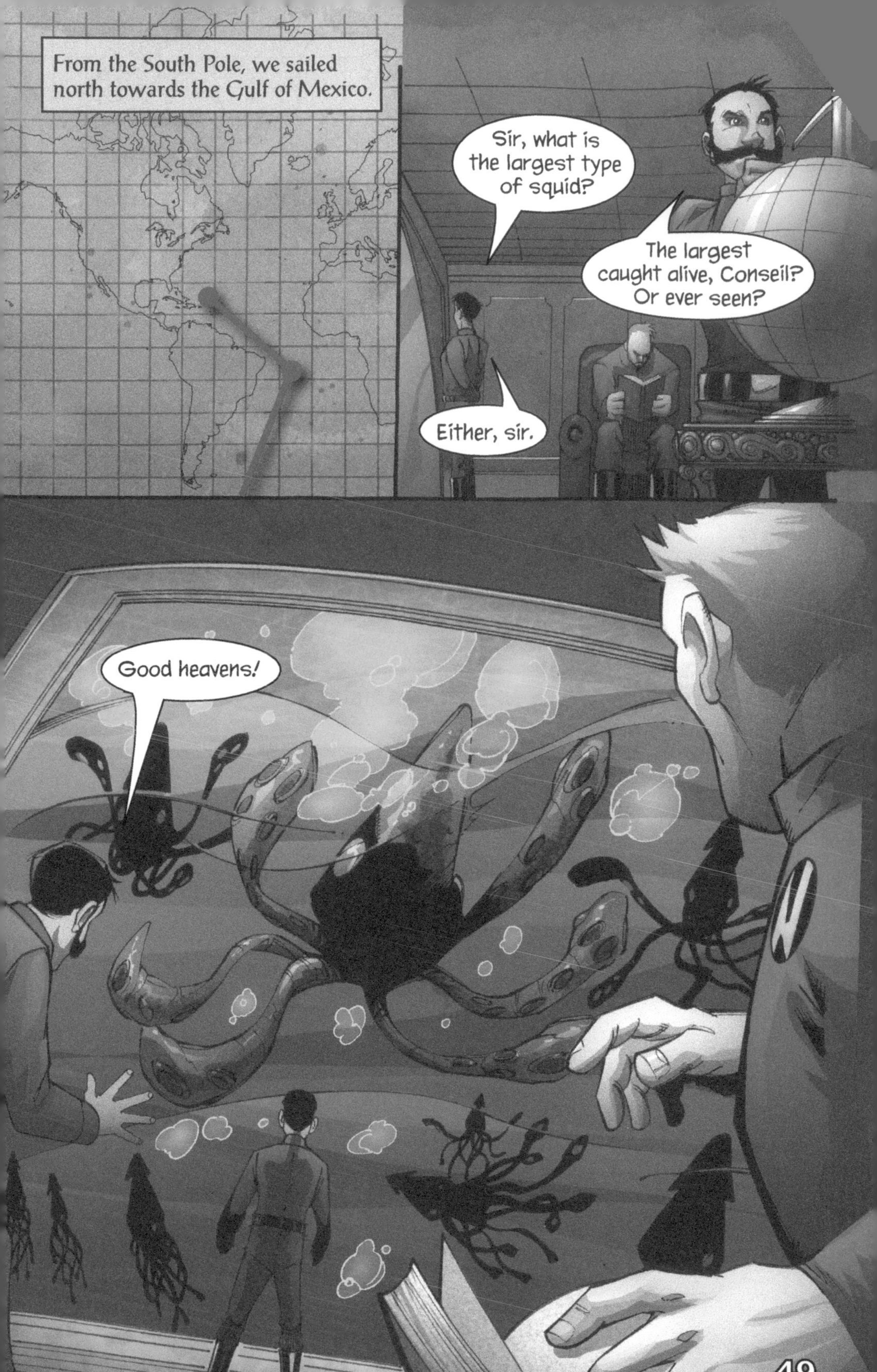
From the South Pole, we sailed north towards the Gulf of Mexico.
Sir, what is the largest type of squid?
The largest caught alive, Conseil? Or ever seen?
Either, sir.
Good heavens!

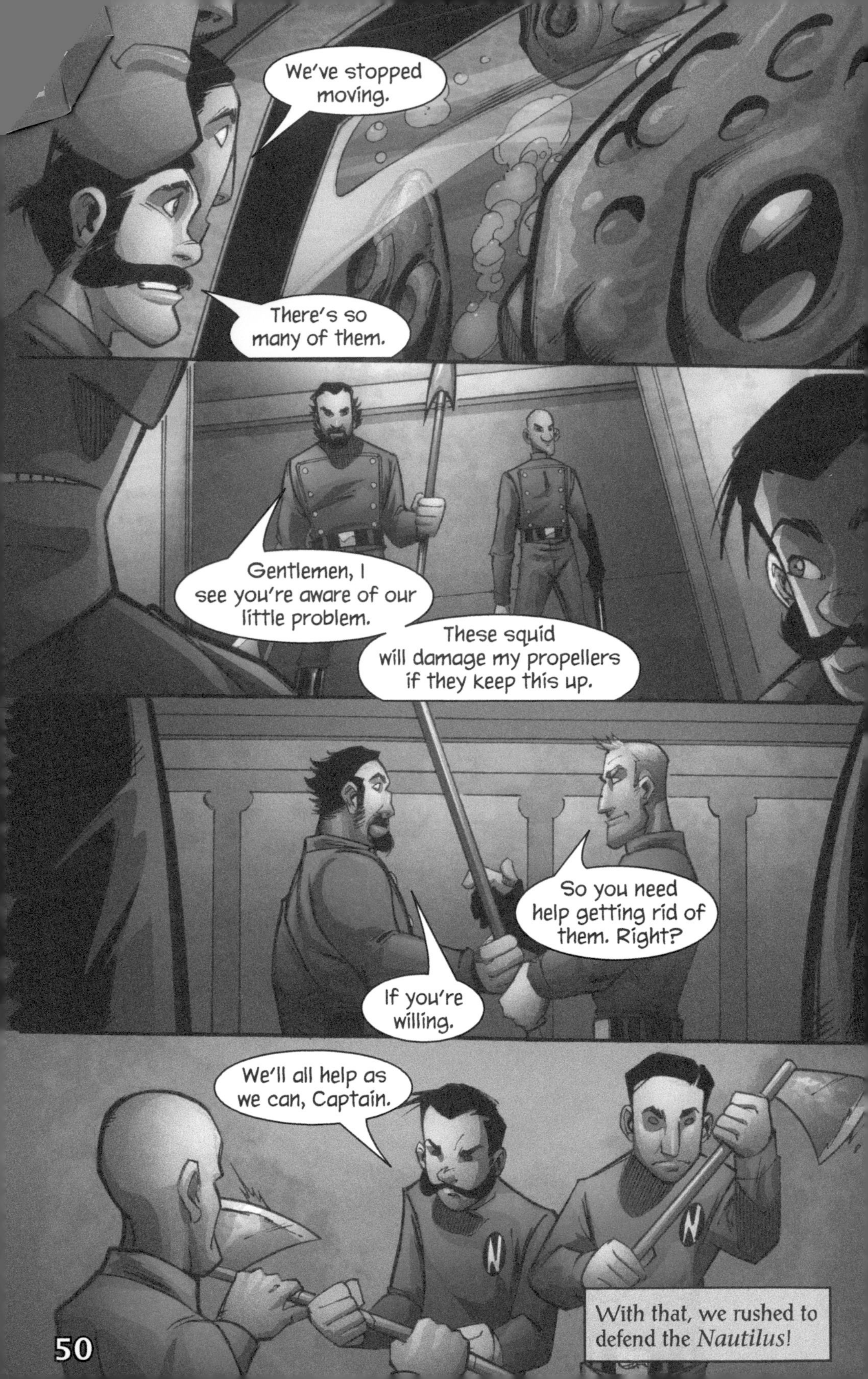
We've stopped moving.
There's so many of them.
Gentlemen, I see you're aware of our little problem.
These squid will damage my propellers if they keep this up.
So you need help getting rid of them. Right?
If you're willing.
We'll all help as we can, Captain.
With that, we rushed to defend the *Nautilus*!

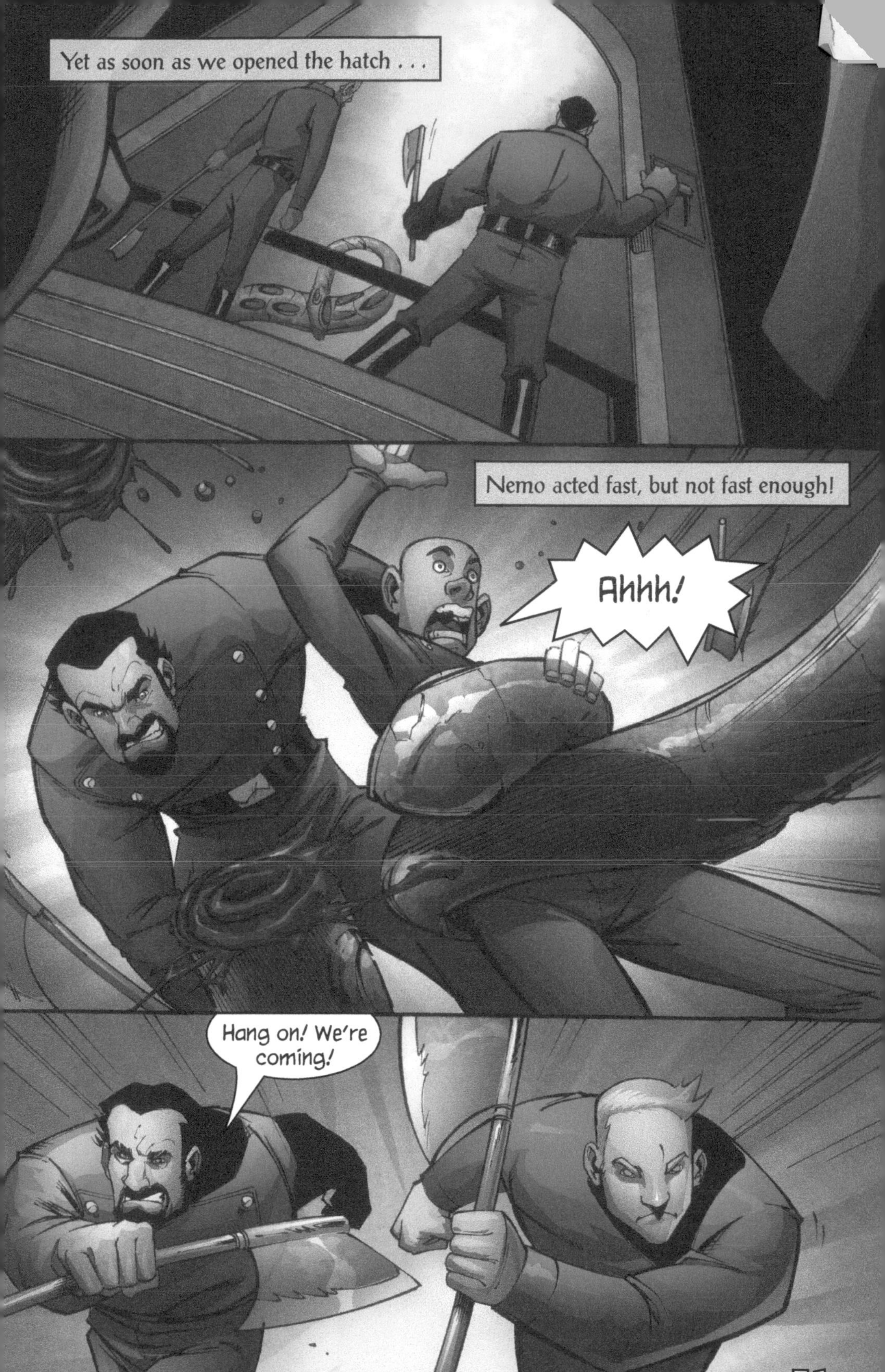
Yet as soon as we opened the hatch . . .
Nemo acted fast, but not fast enough!
Ahhh!
Hang on! We're coming!

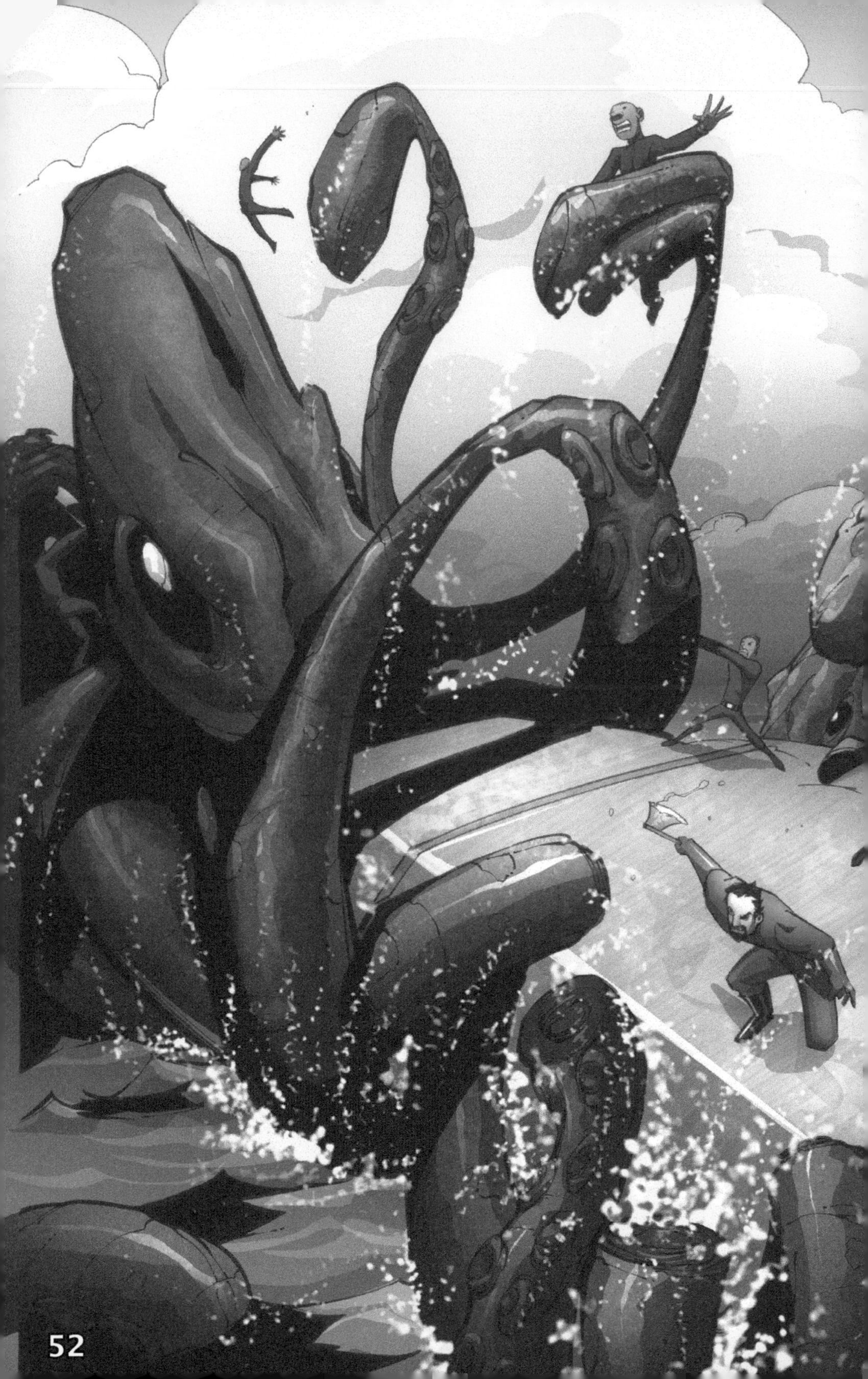

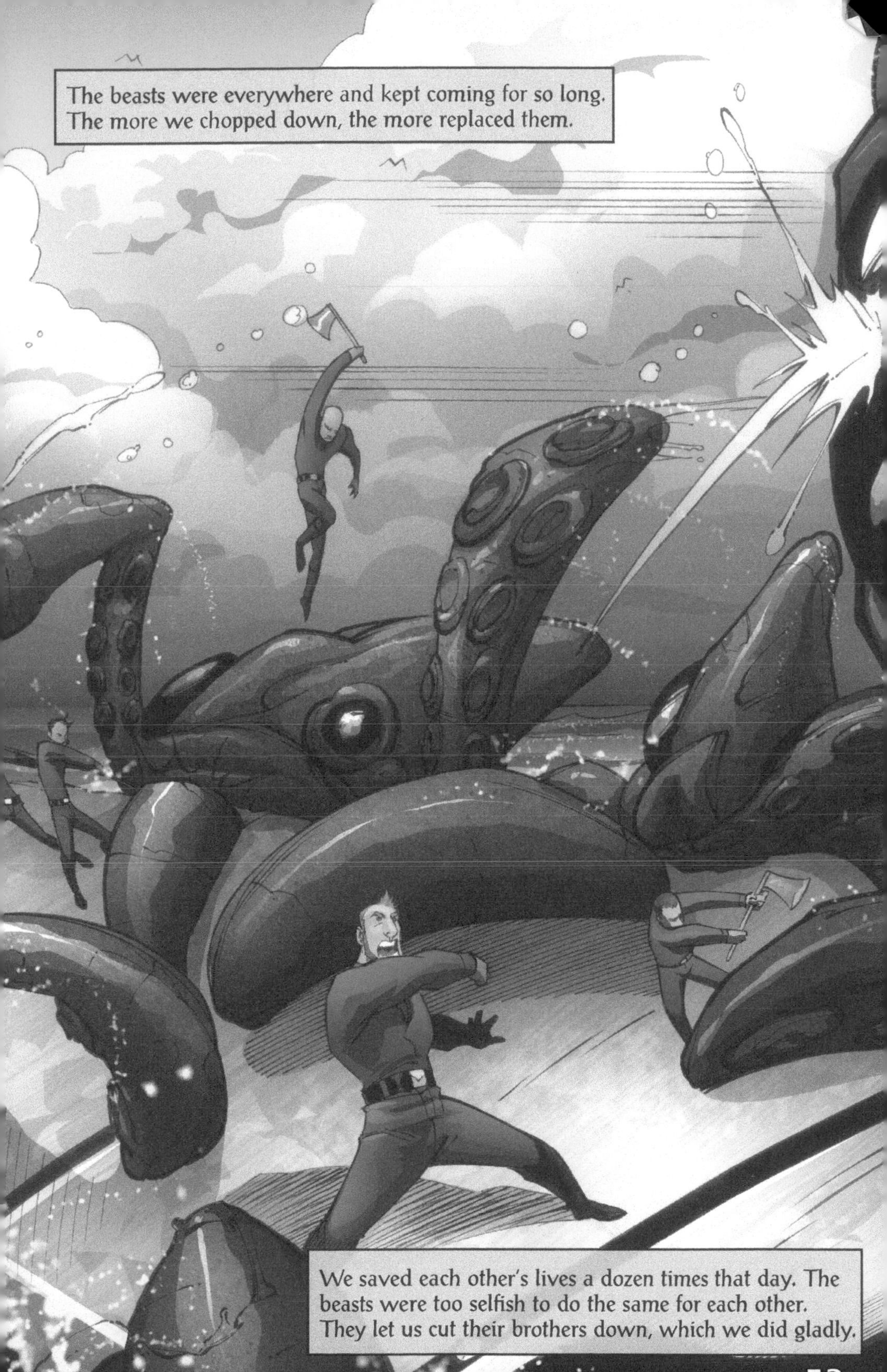
The beasts were everywhere and kept coming for so long. The more we chopped down, the more replaced them.
We saved each other's lives a dozen times that day. The beasts were too selfish to do the same for each other. They let us cut their brothers down, which we did gladly.

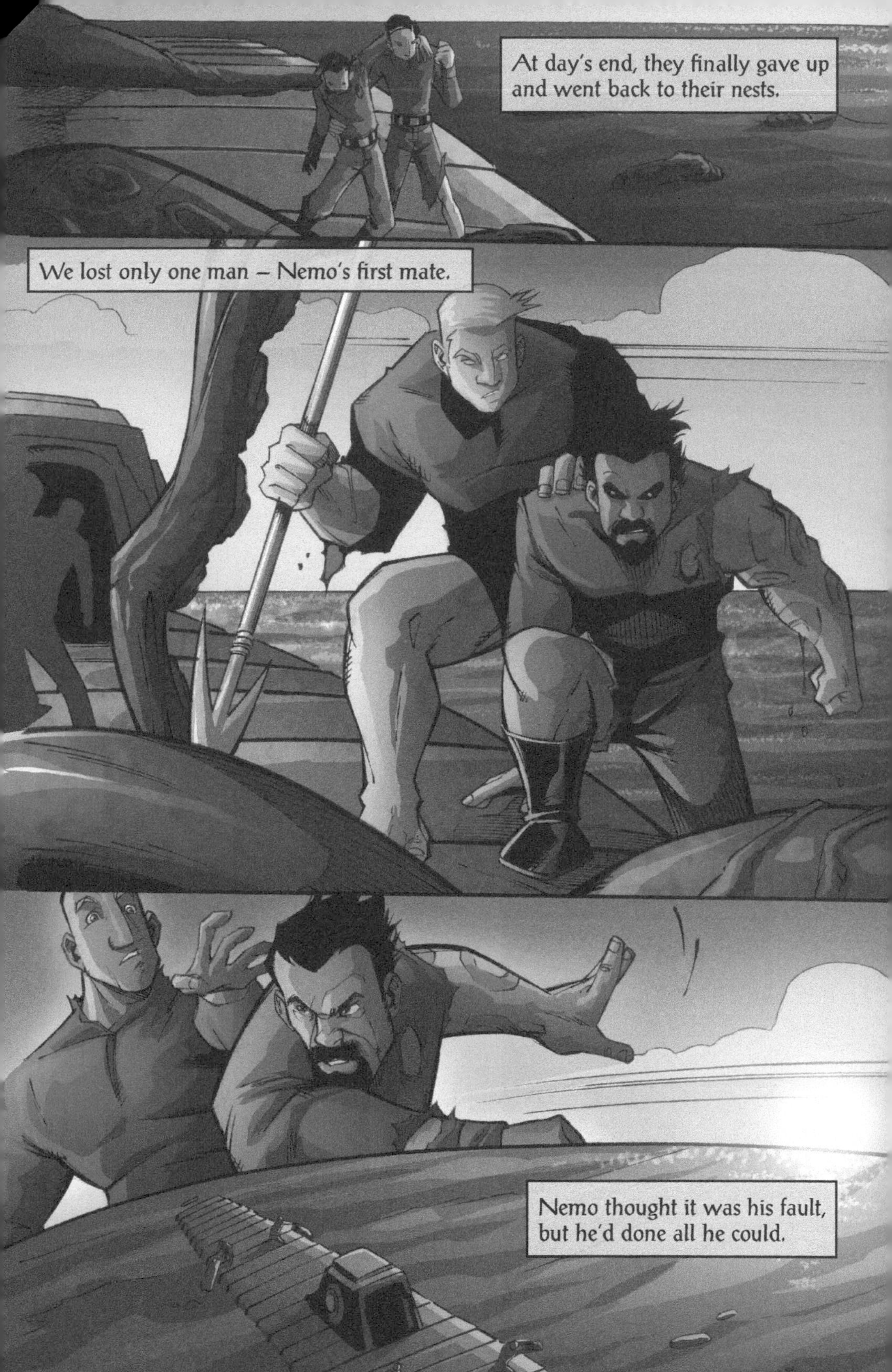
At day's end, they finally gave up and went back to their nests.
We lost only one man – Nemo's first mate.
Nemo thought it was his fault, but he'd done all he could.

CHAPTER 5 : The Voyage Ends

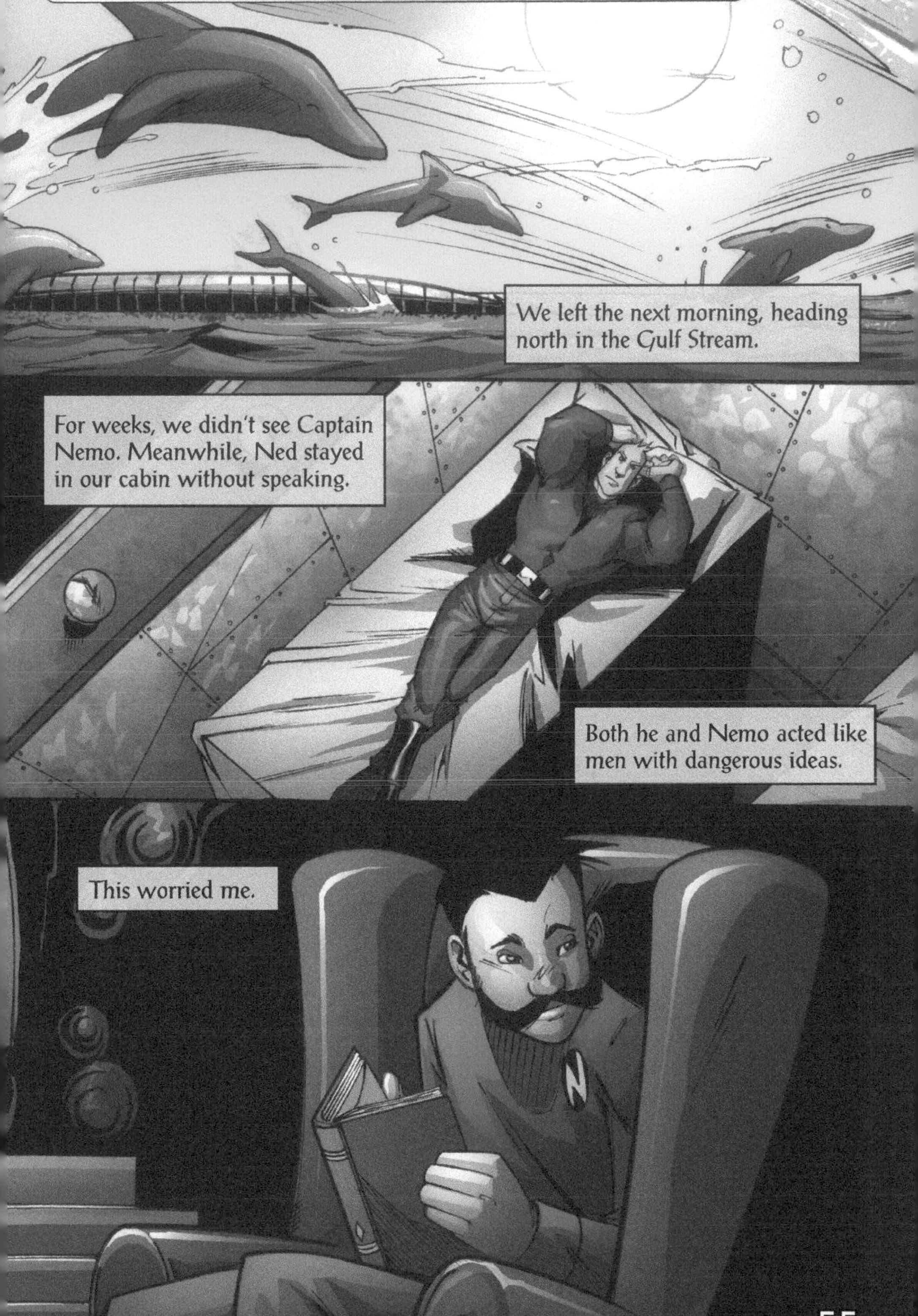

We left the next morning, heading north in the Gulf Stream.
For weeks, we didn't see Captain Nemo. Meanwhile, Ned stayed in our cabin without speaking.
Both he and Nemo acted like men with dangerous ideas.
This worried me.

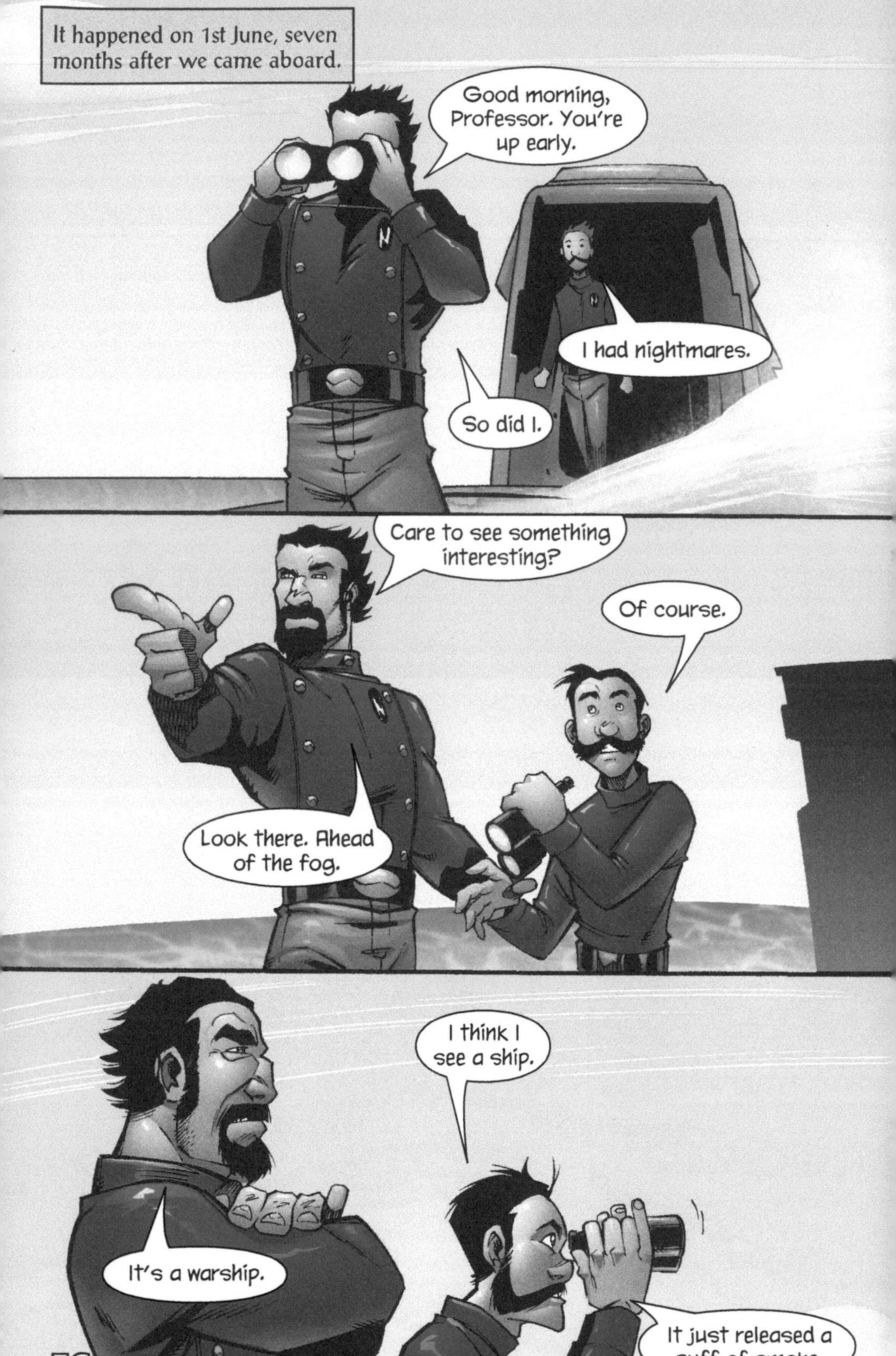

It happened on 1st June, seven months after we came aboard.
Good morning, Professor. You're up early.
I had nightmares.
So did I.
Care to see something interesting?
Of course.
Look there. Ahead of the fog.
I think I see a ship.
It's a warship.
It just released a puff of smoke.

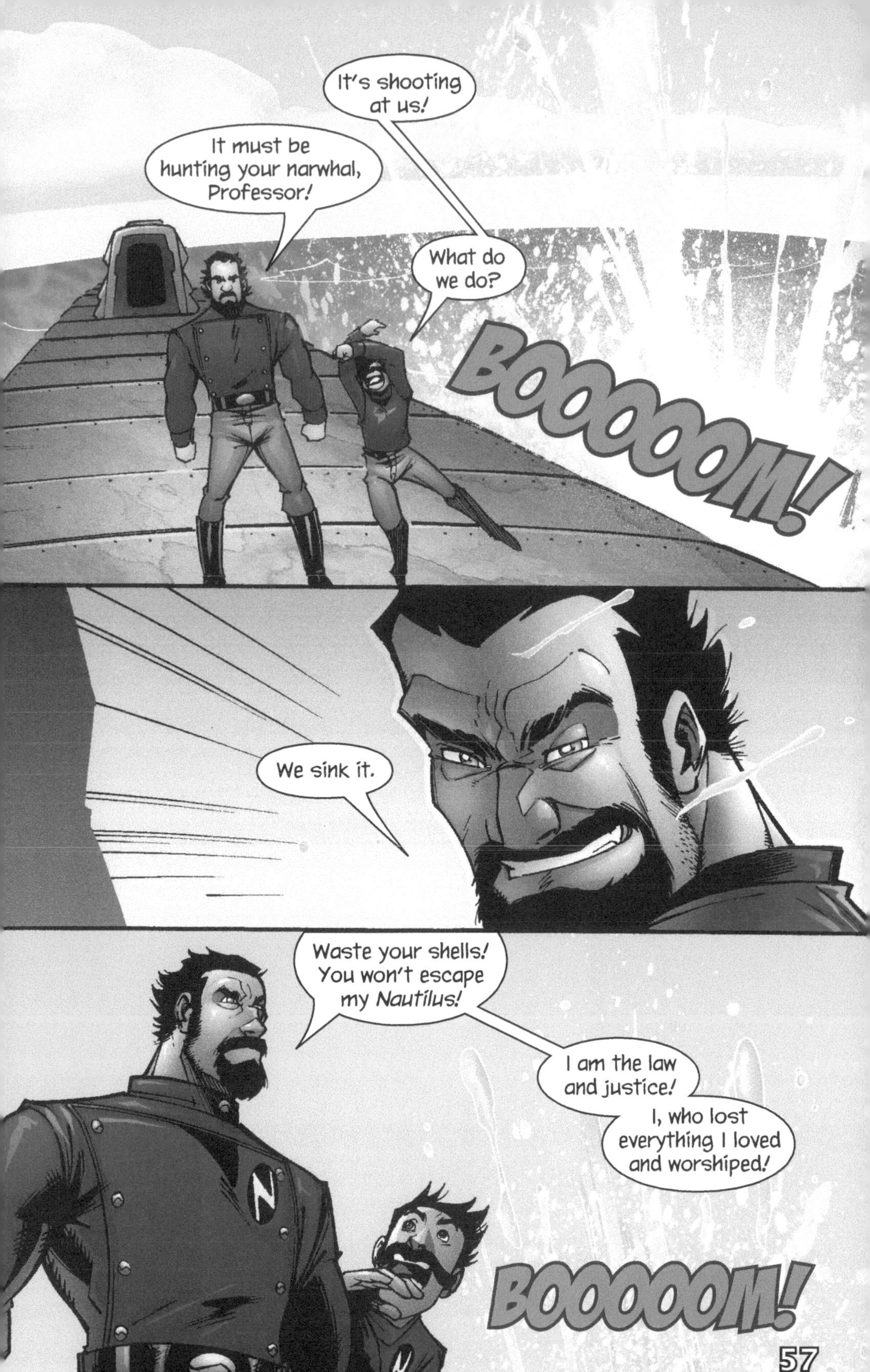
It must be hunting your narwhal, Professor!
It's shooting at us!
What do we do?
BOOOOOM!
We sink it.
Waste your shells! You won't escape my *Nautilus*!
I am the law and justice!
I, who lost everything I loved and worshiped!
BOOOOOM!

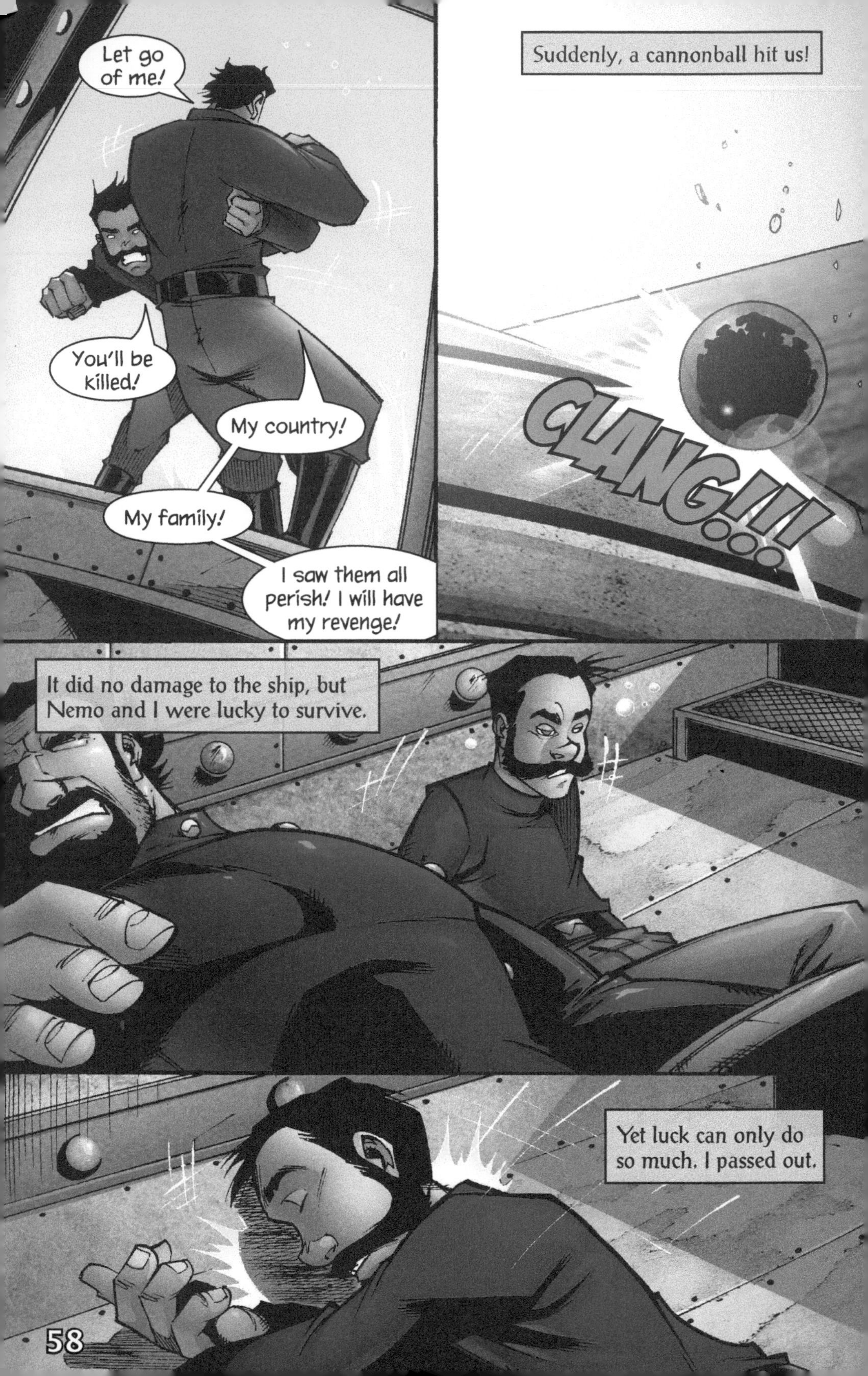

Let go of me!
You'll be killed!
My country!
My family!
I saw them all perish! I will have my revenge!
Suddenly, a cannonball hit us!
CLANG...!!!
It did no damage to the ship, but Nemo and I were lucky to survive.
Yet luck can only do so much. I passed out.

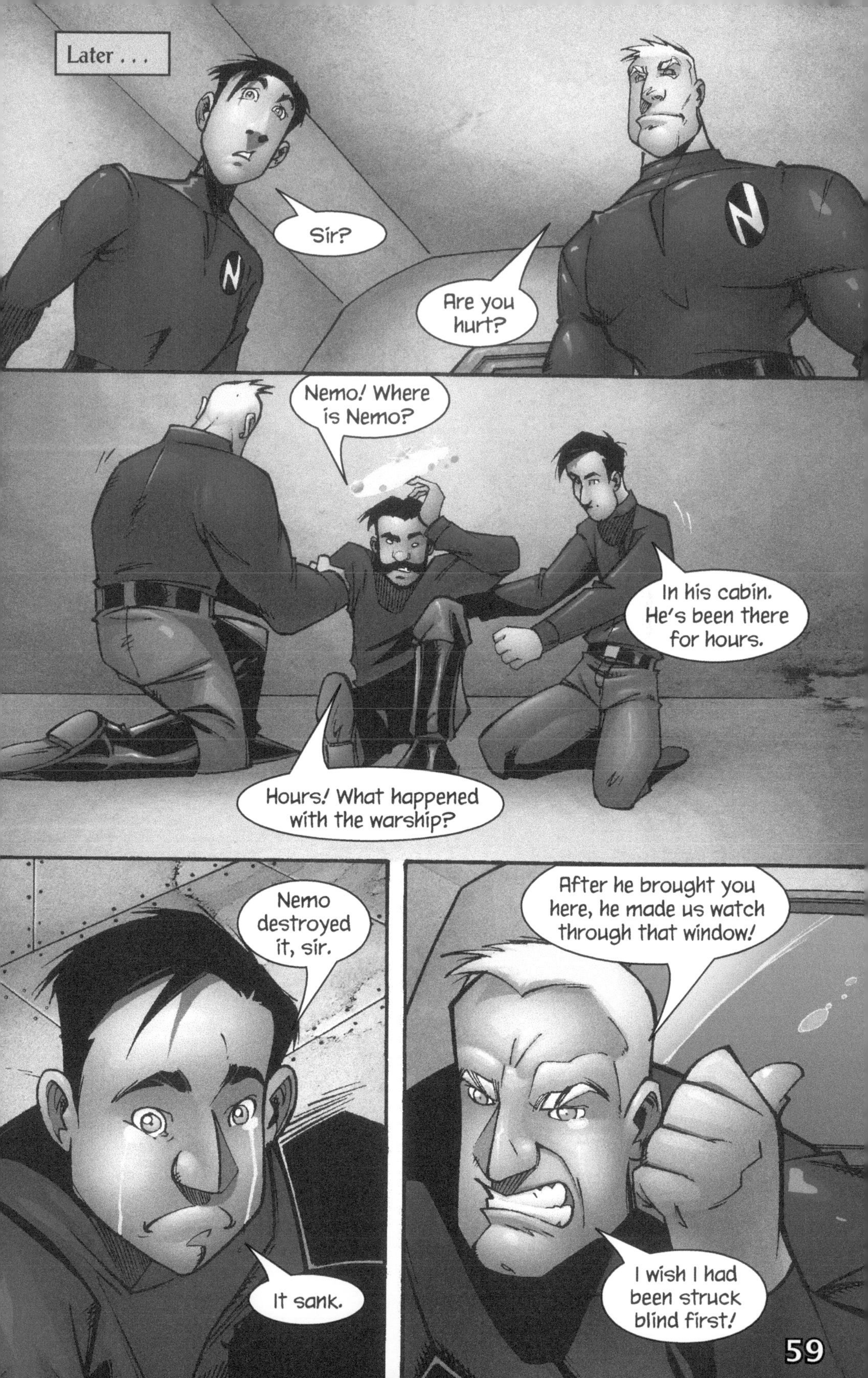
Later . . .
Sir?
Are you hurt?
Nemo! Where is Nemo?
In his cabin. He's been there for hours.
Hours! What happened with the warship?
Nemo destroyed it, sir.
It sank.
After he brought you here, he made us watch through that window!
I wish I had been struck blind first!

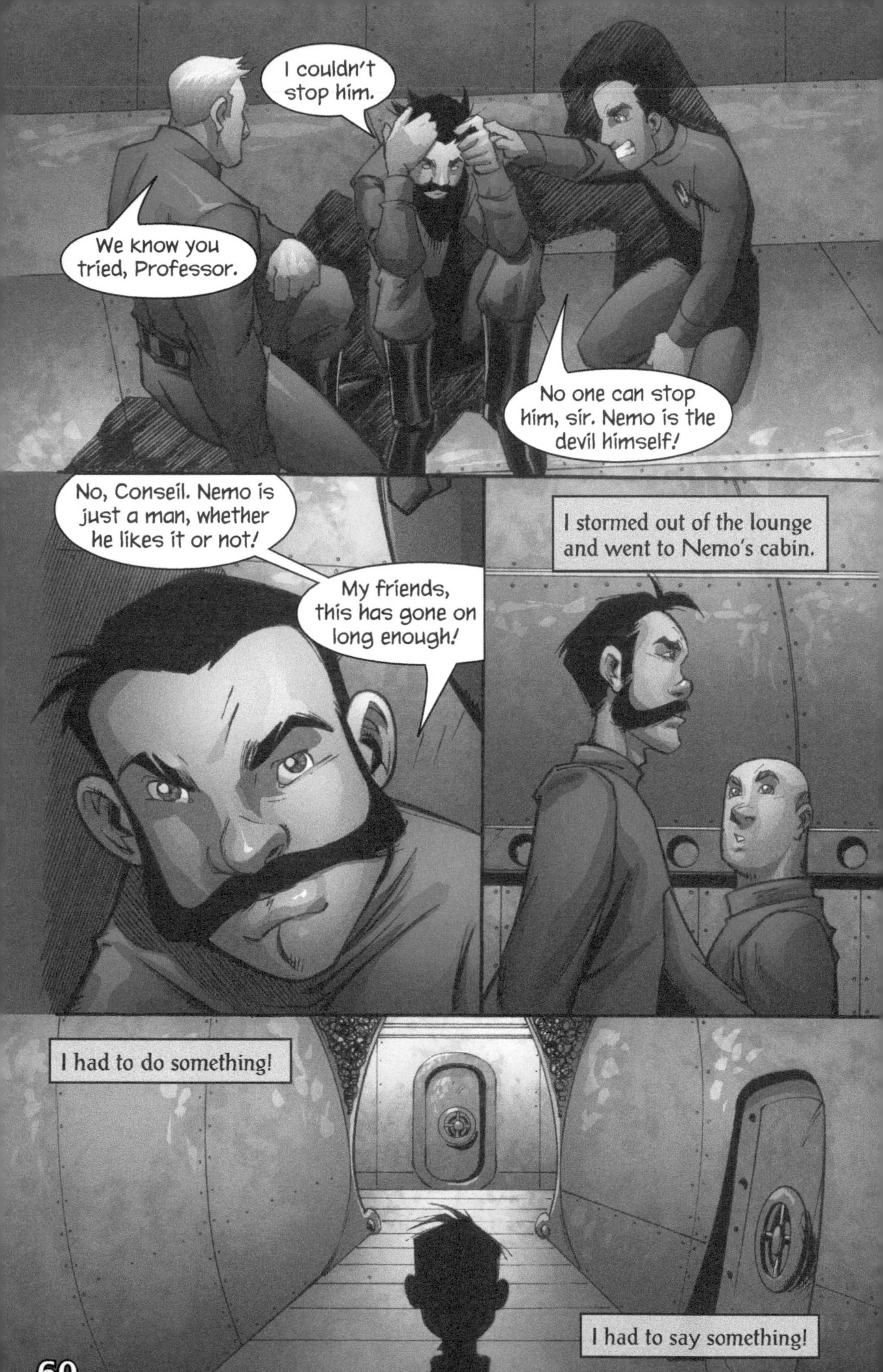
I couldn't stop him.
We know you tried, Professor.
No one can stop him, sir. Nemo is the devil himself!
No, Conseil. Nemo is just a man, whether he likes it or not!
My friends, this has gone on long enough!
I stormed out of the lounge and went to Nemo's cabin.
I had to do something!
I had to say something!

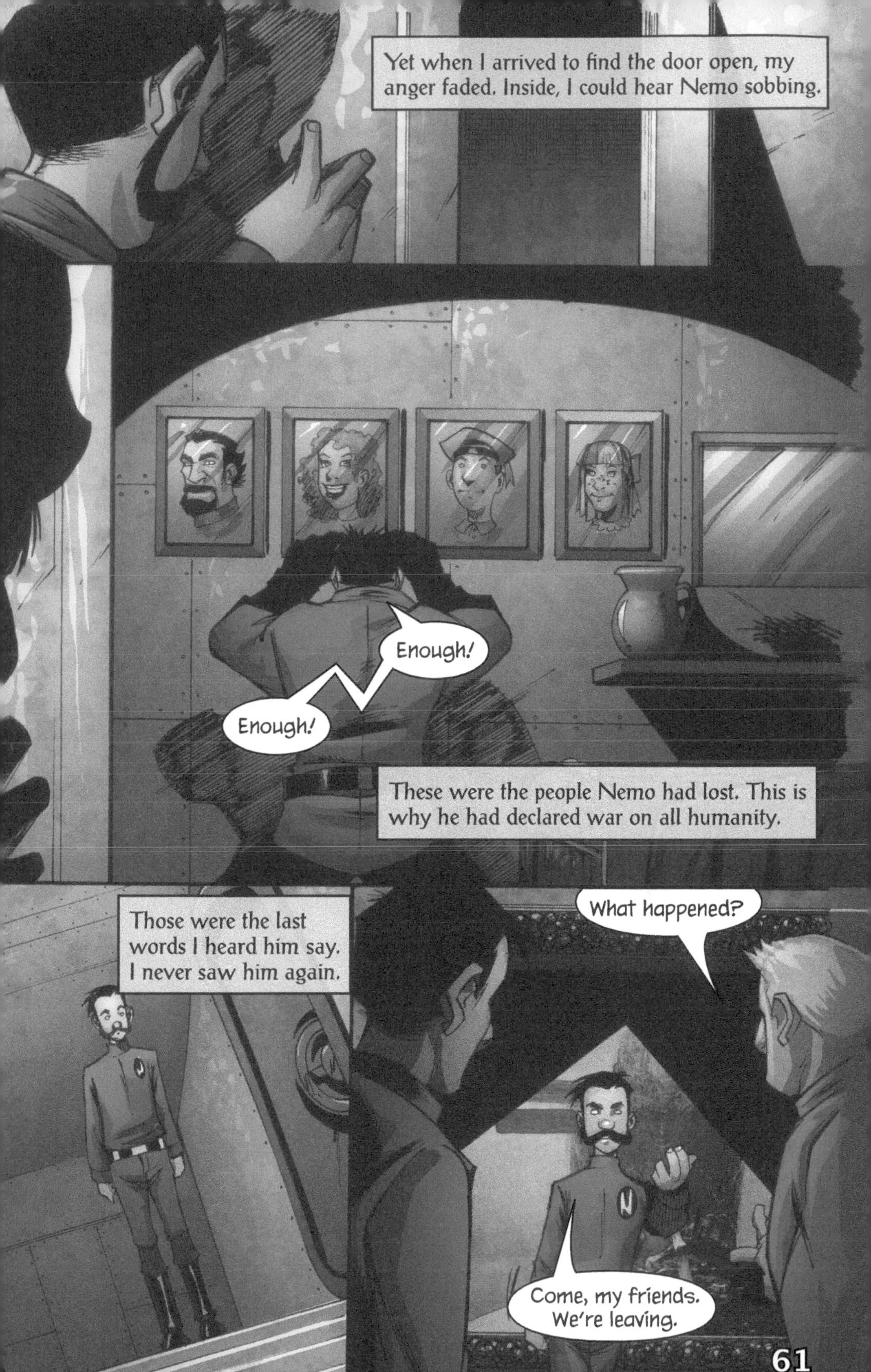
Yet when I arrived to find the door open, my anger faded. Inside, I could hear Nemo sobbing.
Enough!
Enough!
These were the people Nemo had lost. This is why he had declared war on all humanity.
Those were the last words I heard him say. I never saw him again.
What happened?
Come, my friends. We're leaving.

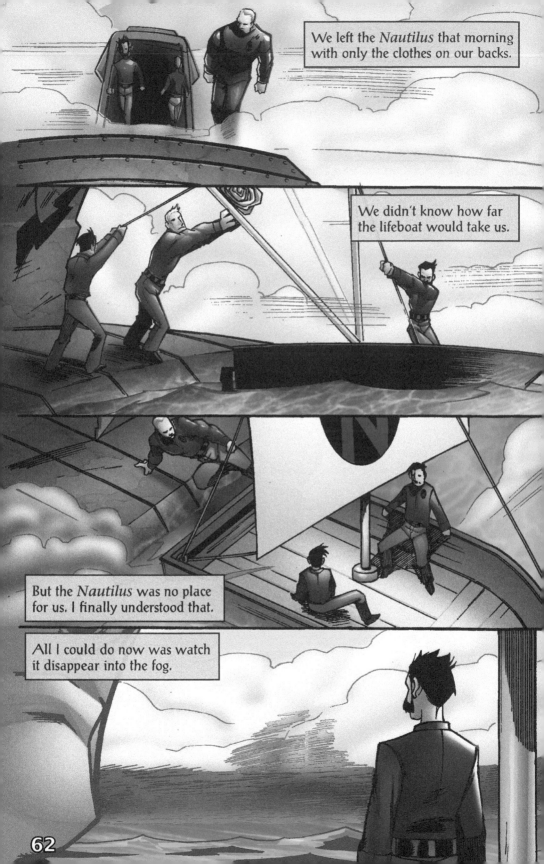

We left the *Nautilus* that morning with only the clothes on our backs.

We didn't know how far the lifeboat would take us.

But the *Nautilus* was no place for us. I finally understood that.

All I could do now was watch it disappear into the fog.

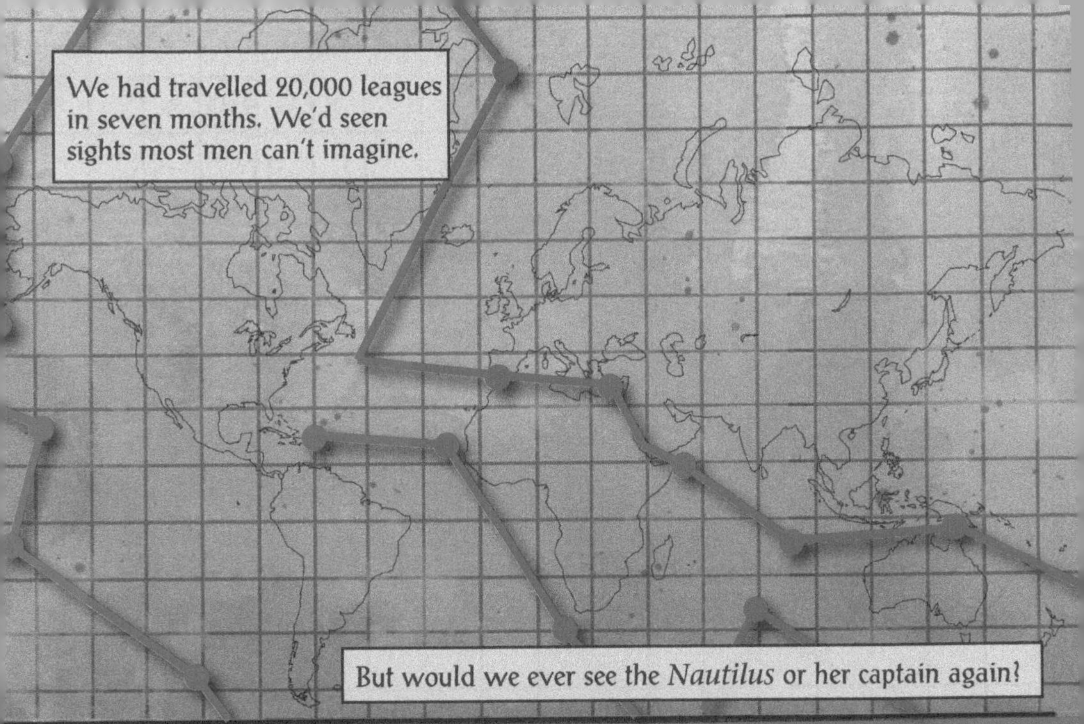
We had travelled 20,000 leagues in seven months. We'd seen sights most men can't imagine.
But would we ever see the *Nautilus* or her captain again?

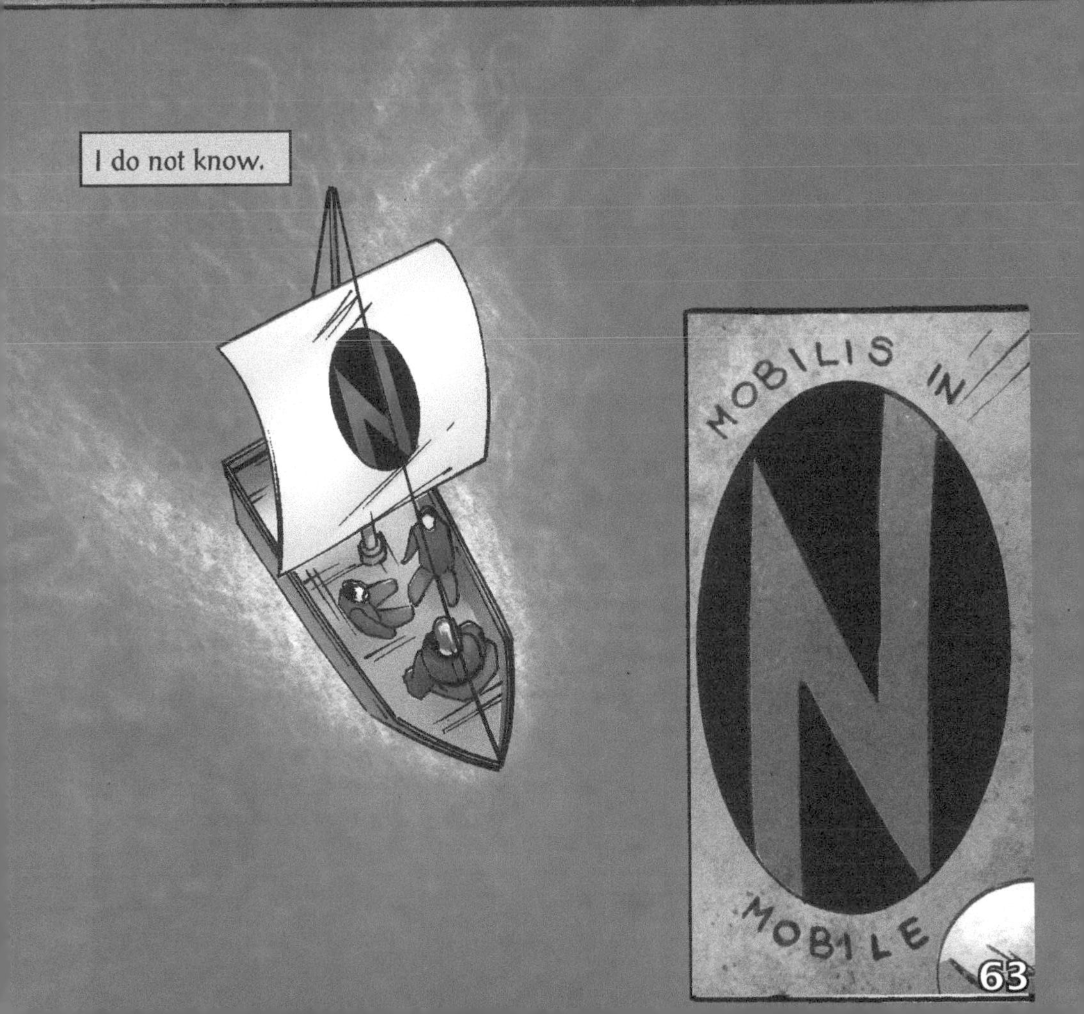
I do not know.
MOBILIS IN MOBILE

ABOUT THE AUTHOR

Jules Verne was born on 8 February, 1828, in France. Growing up near a river, the constant sight of ships sparked his interest in travel. As a young man, Verne even tried to run away and become a cabin boy. Fortunately, his father caught him, and soon Verne was off to study law in Paris. While there, Verne escaped the boredom of his studies by writing stories. When his father found out about this hobby, he stopped sending money for school. Verne started selling his stories, many of which became popular, including *20,000 Leagues Under the Sea* in 1870. Before he died in 1905, the author bought a boat and sailed around Europe.

ABOUT THE RETELLING AUTHOR

Carl Bowen is a writer and editor who lives in Georgia, USA. He was born in Louisiana, lived briefly in England and was raised in Georgia where he attended grammar school, high school, and college. He has published a handful of novels and more than a dozen short stories, all while working at White Wolf Publishing as an editor and advertising copywriter. His first graphic novel, published by Udon Entertainment, is called *Exalted*. This book, *20,000 Leagues Under the Sea*, is his first book for Stone Arch Books.

GLOSSARY

binoculars (bih-NOK-yuh-lurz) – an instrument people look through to make distant objects appear closer

canal (kah-NAL) – a passageway that connects two bodies of water

chamber (CHAYM-bur) – a small room or closed-in space

civilized (SIV-i-lized) – having manners and an education

harpoon (har-POON) – a large spear often used to hunt fish or whales

humanity (hyoo-MAN-ih-tee) – all human beings

justice (JUHSS-tiss) – a judge or someone that enforces a set of rules or laws

league (LEEG) – a unit of measurement; one **league** equals about five kilometers (three miles).

lounge (LOUNJ) – a room where people can relax, such as a living room

mobilis in mobile (MOH-bee-leess IN MOH-bee-lay) – a Latin phrase meaning "moving through moving waters"

narwhal (NAHR-wol) – a whalelike, ocean animal about 20 feet long with long, spirally twisted tusks

theory (THEER-ee) – an idea that explains the reason for something

DIVE DEEPER
INTO SUBMARINES

Many people believe Alexander the Great was the first person to journey underwater in a contained vessel. Legend says the Greek leader explored the Aegean Sea inside a glass barrel around 333 BCE, more than 2,000 years ago.

Artist Leonardo Da Vinci, who painted the famous *Mona Lisa,* also worked on plans to build an underwater ship during the 1500s. However, Da Vinci kept his plans a secret because he feared the invention would be used for war.

Less than 300 years later, Da Vinci's prediction came true. David Bushnell built the first submarine used for battle. The *Turtle,* as it was called, was made of wood, held one person, and could stay under water for half an hour. On 6 September, 1776, the American army used the *Turtle* against a British warship. The attack was unsuccessful.

During the Civil War, the United States Navy tested their first submarine. The *Alligator* measured 14 metres long and could hold more than 14 crew members. While being towed into battle in 1863, a storm sunk the sub off the North Carolina coast. It has never been found.

Early subs were often powered by oars or hand-cranked propellers. The United States Navy launched the first nuclear-powered submarine in 1954. It was named the *Nautilus,* the same as Captain Nemo's underwater vessel. In 1958, the *Nautilus* became the first sub to cross beneath the North Pole.

Nuclear energy has since powered some of the fastest subs ever built, including Russia's Alfa class submarines. These subs could travel nearly 480 kilometres per hour!

On January 23, 1960, *Trieste* became the deepest-diving underwater vessel ever built. The *Trieste* dove nearly 11,600 metres before reaching the floor of the Pacific Ocean.

DISCUSSION QUESTIONS

1. If you were trapped in Nemo's submarine, would you want to escape like Ned Land, or would you enjoy the ride? Explain your answer.

2. Ned Land didn't seem to trust Captain Nemo. So, why do you think he saved Nemo from the shark? Explain your answer using details from the story.

3. Do you think Captain Nemo will ever get over the people he has lost and return to the surface? Or, do you think he will spend the rest of his life at sea? Why?

WRITING PROMPTS

1. Write your own underwater adventure. What would your submarine look like? Where would you travel? What type of creatures would you face?

2. At the end of the story, the *Nautilus* submarine disappears into the fog. Where do you think it will go next? Write a story about another voyage with Nemo and his crew.

3. Imagine you were going on a year-long underwater voyage and could only pack three things. What three things would you take with you and why?

OTHER BOOKS

BRAM STOKER'S
DRACULA
GRAPHIC NOVEL

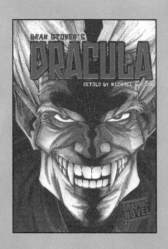

Dracula

On a business trip to Transylvania, Jonathan Harker stays at an eerie castle owned by a man named Count Dracula. When strange things start to happen, Harker investigates and finds the count sleeping in a coffin! Harker isn't safe, and when the count escapes to London, neither are his friends.

GRAPHIC NOVEL
Jonathan Swift's
GULLIVER'S TRAVELS

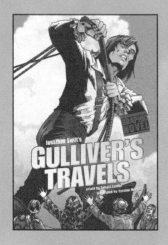

Gulliver's Travels

Lemuel Gulliver always dreamed of sailing across seas, but he never could have imagined the places his travels would take him. On the island of Lilliput, he is captured by tiny creatures no more than six inches tall. In a country of Blefuscu, he is nearly squashed by an army of giants. His adventures could be the greatest tales ever told, if he survives long enough to tell them.

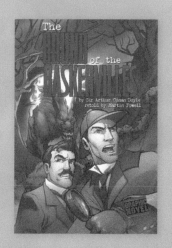

The
HOUND of the
BASKERVILLES
by Sir Arthur Conan Doyle
retold by Martin Powell
GRAPHIC NOVEL

The Hound of the Baskervilles

Late one night, Sir Charles Baskerville is attacked outside his castle in Dartmoor, Devon. Could it be the Hound of the Baskervilles, a legendary creature that haunts the nearby moor? Sherlock Holmes, the world's greatest detective, is on the case.

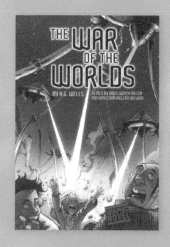

THE WAR OF THE WORLDS
BY H.G. WELLS
GRAPHIC NOVEL

The War of the Worlds

In the late 19th century, a cylinder crashes down near London. When George investigates, a Martian activates an evil machine and begins destroying everything in its path! George must find a way to survive a War of the Worlds.

GRAPHIC REVOLVE

If you have enjoyed this story, there are many more exciting tales for you to discover in the Graphic Revolve collection...

20,000 Leagues Under the Sea

Black Beauty

Dracula

Frankenstein

Gulliver's Travels

The Hound of the Baskervilles

The Hunchback of Notre Dame

King Arthur and the Knights of the Round Table

Robin Hood

The Strange Case of Dr Jekyll and Mr Hyde

Treasure Island

The War of the Worlds